HANDBOOK OF FLORICULTURE

By

Dr. Pooja

Deptt. of Botany
R.C.C. College
Ghaziabad (U.P.)
(India)

DPH

DISCOVERY PUBLISHING HOUSE PVT. LTD.
NEW DELHI-110 002

Published by:
Tilak Wasan
DISCOVERY PUBLISHING HOUSE PVT. LTD.
4383/4A, Ansari Road, Darya Ganj
New Delhi-110 002 (India)
Phone : +91-11-23279245, 43596064-65
Fax : +91-11-23253475
E-mail : parul.wasan@gmail.com
discoverypublishinghouse@gmail.com
web : www.discoverypublishinggroup.com

***First Edition:* 2012**
ISBN: 978-93-5056-092-1

Handbook of Floriculture

Printed at:
Shree Balaji Art Press
Delhi

Preface

Floriculture, or flower farming, is a discipline of horticulture concerned with the cultivation of flowering and ornamental plants for gardens and for floristry, comprising the floral industry. The development plant breeding of new varieties is a major occupation of floriculturists.

Floriculture crops include bedding plants, flowering plants, foliage plants or houseplants, cut cultivated greens, and cut flowers. As distinguished from nursery crops, floriculture crops are generally herbaceous. Bedding and garden plants consist of young flowering plants (annuals and perennials) and vegetable plants. They are grown in cell packs (in flats or trays), in pots, or in hanging baskets, usually inside a controlled environment, and sold largely for gardens and landscaping. Geraniums, impatiens, and petunias are the best-selling bedding plants. Chrysanthemums are the major perennial garden plant in the United States.

Flowering plants are largely sold in pots for indoor use. The major flowering plants are poinsettias, orchids, florist chrysanthemums, and finished florist azaleas. Foliage plants are also sold in pots and hanging baskets for indoor and patio use, including larger specimens for office, hotel, and restaurant interiors.

Cut flowers are usually sold in bunches or as bouquets with cut foliage. The production of cut flowers is specifically known as the cut flower industry. Farming flowers and foliage employs special aspects of floriculture, such as spacing, training and pruning plants for optimal flower harvest; and post-harvest treatment such as chemical treatments, storage, preservation and packaging. In Australia and the United States some species are harvested from the wild for the cut flower market.

Floristry is the general term used to describe the professional floral trade. It encompasses flower care and handling, floral design or flower arranging, merchandising, and display and flower delivery. Wholesale florists sell bulk flowers and related supplies to professionals in the trade. Retail florists offer fresh flowers and related products and services to consumers.

Floristry is a term that refers to the cultivation of flowers as well as their arrangement, and to the business of selling them. However, the floral industry is the basic drive behind floristry. Florist shops, along with online stores are the main flower-only outlets, but supermarkets, garden supply stores and filling stations also sell flowers.

Floral design or floral arts is the art of creating flower arrangements in vases, bowls, baskets or other containers, or making bouquets and compositions from cut flowers, foliages, herbs, ornamental grasses and other botanical materials. Often the terms 'floral design' and 'floristry' are considered synonymous. Florists are people who work with flowers and plants, generally at the retail level. The term is not to be confused with floristics (the study of distribution and relationships of plant species over geographic areas). Floristry is also not to be confused with horticulture which more broadly relates to the cultivation of flowers and plants.

Author

Contents

1 Introduction

Floriculture, or *flower farming*, is a discipline of horticulture concerned with the cultivation of flowering and ornamental plants for gardens and for floristry, comprising the floral industry. The development plant breeding of new varieties is a major occupation of floriculturists.

Floriculture crops include bedding plants, flowering plants, foliage plants or houseplants, cut cultivated greens, and cut flowers. As distinguished from nursery crops, floriculture crops are generally herbaceous. Bedding and garden plants consist of young flowering plants (annuals and perennials) and vegetable plants. They are grown in cell packs (in flats or trays), in pots, or in hanging baskets, usually inside a controlled environment, and sold largely for gardens and landscaping. Geraniums, impatiens, and petunias are the best-selling bedding plants. Chrysanthemums are the major perennial garden plants in the United States.

Flowering plants are largely sold in pots for indoor use. The major flowering plants are poinsettias, orchids, florist chrysanthemums, and finished florist azaleas. Foliage plants are also sold in pots and hanging baskets for indoor and patio use, including larger specimens for office, hotel, and restaurant interiors.

Cut flowers are usually sold in bunches or as bouquets with cut foliage. The production of cut flowers is specifically known as the *cut flower industry*. Farming flowers and foliage employs special aspects of floriculture, such as spacing, training and pruning plants for optimal flower harvest; and post-harvest treatment such as chemical treatments, storage, preservation and packaging. In Australia and the United States some species are harvested from the wild for the cut flower market.

Horticulture is the industry and science of plant cultivation including the process of preparing soil for the planting of seeds, tubers, or cuttings. Horticulturists work and conduct research in the disciplines of plant propagation and cultivation, crop production, plant breeding and genetic engineering, plant biochemistry, and plant physiology. The work particularly involves fruits, berries, nuts, vegetables, flowers, trees, shrubs, and turf. Horticulturists work to improve crop yield, quality, nutritional value, and resistance to insects, diseases, and environmental stresses. Horticulture usually refers to gardening on a smaller scale, while agriculture refers to the large-scale cultivation of crops. The word is composite, from two words, horti, meaning grass, originating in the Greek , meaning the same (grass) and the word culture.

Horticulture involves eight areas of study, which can be grouped into two broad sections — ornamentals and edibles:

- Arboriculture is the study of, and the selection, planting, care, and removal of, individual trees, shrubs, vines, and other perennial woody plants;
- Floriculture includes the production and marketing of floral crops;
- Landscape horticulture includes the production, marketing and maintenance of landscape plants;
- Olericulture includes the production and marketing of vegetables;

- Pomology includes the production and marketing of fruits;
- Viticulture includes the production and marketing of grapes;
- Post-harvest physiology involves maintaining the quality of and preventing the spoilage of horticultural crops;
- Horticulturists can work in industry, government or educational institutions or private collections. They can be cropping systems engineers, wholesale or retail business managers, propagators and tissue culture specialists (fruits, vegetables, ornamentals, and turf), crop inspectors, crop production advisers, extension specialists, plant breeders, research scientists, and of course, teachers.

Disciplines which complement horticulture include biology, botany, entomology, chemistry, mathematics, genetics, physiology, statistics, computer science, and communications, garden design, planting design. Plant science and horticulture courses include: plant materials, plant propagation, tissue culture, crop production, post-harvest handling, plant breeding, pollination management, crop nutrition, entomology, plant pathology, economics, and business. Some careers in horticultural science require a masters (MS) or doctoral (Ph.D) degree.

Horticulture is practiced in many gardens, "plant growth centres" and nurseries. Activities in nurseries range from preparing seeds and cuttings to growing fully mature plants. These are often sold or transferred to ornamental gardens or market gardens.

Horticulture has a very long history. The study and science of horticulture dates all the way back to the times of Alexander the Great, and has been going on ever since, with present day horticulturists such as Freeman S. Howlett, the revolutionary horticulturist. The origins of horticulture lie in the transition of human communities from nomadic hunter-gatherers to sedentary or semi-sedentary horticultural communities, cultivating a variety of crops on a small scale around their dwellings or in specialized plots visited occasionally during migrations from one area to the next. (such as the 'milpa' or maize field of Mesoamerican cultures). In forest areas such horticulture is often carried out in swiddens ('slash and burn' areas). A characteristic of horticultural communities is that useful trees are often to be found planted around communities or specially retained from the natural ecosystem.

Horticulture primarily differs from agriculture in two ways, firstly it generally encompasses a smaller scale of cultivation, using small plots of mixed crops rather than large fields of single crops. Secondly horticultural cultivations generally include a wide variety of crops, even including fruit trees with ground crops. Agricultural cultivations however as a rule focus on one primary crop. In pre-contact North America the semi-sedentary horticultural communities of the Eastern Woodlands (growing maize, squash and sunflower) contrasted markedly with the mobile hunter-gatherer communities of the Plains people. In Central America, Maya horticulture involved augmentation of the forest with useful trees such as papaya, avocado, cacao, ceiba and sapodilla. In the cornfields, multiple crops were grown such as beans (using cornstalks as supports), squash, pumpkins and chilli peppers, in some cultures tended mainly or exclusively by women.

Floristry is the general term used to describe the professional floral trade. It encompasses flower care and handling, floral design or flower arranging, merchandising, and display and flower delivery. Wholesale florists sell bulk flowers and related supplies to professionals in the trade. Retail florists offer fresh flowers and related products and services to consumers.

Floristry is a term that refers to the cultivation of flowers as well as their arrangement, and to the business of selling them. However, the floral industry is the basic drive behind floristry. Florist shops, along with online stores are the main flower-only outlets, but supermarkets, garden supply stores and filling stations also sell flowers.

Floral design or floral arts is the art of creating flower arrangements in vases, bowls, baskets or other containers, or making bouquets and compositions from cut flowers, foliages, herbs, ornamental grasses and other botanical materials. Often the terms 'floral design' and 'floristry' are considered synonymous. Florists are people who work with flowers and plants, generally at the retail level. The term is not to be confused with floristics (the study of distribution and relationships of plant species over geographic areas.). Floristry is also not to be confused with horticulture which more broadly relates to the cultivation of flowers and plants.

The craft of floristry, or being a florist, involves various skills and creativity. A florist should be able to select flowers and other floral supplies and materials that will look good together (based on principles and elements of floral design or market demands), know how to handle and arrange flowers and plants so they will remain fresh as long as possible, and would be desirable for purchase, which also involves knowledge of customers' requirements and expectations. Ability to create a variety of floral designs such as wreaths, bouquets, corsages, boutonnières/'buttonholes', permanent arrangements and other more complicated arrangements is also important.

The flowers sold in florist shops typically represent the varieties abundantly available in the season but also include blossoms flown in from around the world. Basic varieties include roses, tulips, irises, orchids and lilies. Fashion sometimes plays a role in floristry; what is considered the flower that everyone needs to have today can change very quickly.

Some shops also stock gift baskets, fruits, and chocolates as well as flowers, whereas some shops will purchase these things only when needed for an order. Floral business is seasonal and is heavily influenced by the following holidays and events: Christmas, Valentine's Day, Administrative Professionals' Day, Mothers' Day, All Souls Day, Advent, Easter, weddings and funerals. These occasions make up the largest part of the business, with the sale of house plants and home decor being a smaller, but more constant, part. Flowers for personal enjoyment as well as those selected to celebrate birthdays, anniversaries, thank-you's and get well wishes are also a significant portion of a florist's business.

Floral education, both formal and informal, is another significant segment of the floral industry. Established floral designers and artists impart their craft to students interested in floral design as hobby or career. Courses are generally available in university horticulture departments, through community colleges, via private post-secondary vocational schools and through professional florist trade associations.

The floral business has been impacted significantly by the corporate and social event world in as much as flowers play a large part in the decor of special events and meetings. Centerpieces, entryways, reception tables, bridal bouquets, wedding chuppahs and stage sets and only a few examples of how flowers are used in the business and social event arenas.

Styles of Floristry

Many nations have their own style of floral arranging:

Ikebana

Ikebana is a style of floral design that originated in Japan. Most well known for its simplicity of line and form, Ikebana is a design style primarily practiced for personal enjoyment.

English Garden

English Garden style is traditionally an English form of floral design. Stems are placed in a radial fashion and feature abundant use of seasonal flowers and foliages. These designs are often done as low, tufted mounds, or taller vase arrangements that are all-sided (360°), and incorporate garden flowers like roses, delphinium and peonies. Many florists that follow this design style do not use Baby's Breath, Carnations and Leatherleaf.

High Style

High Style is a catch-all term to describe contemporary, linear designs that highlights unique forms of both individual floral materials and of the designs themselves. Arrangements generally feature negative space and incorporate asymmetric placement of materials. The style stands in direct contrast to traditional radial arrangements such as English Garden.

High Style designs often incorporate unique, exotic or tropical flowers such as such as Bird of Paradise, Anthurium and Protea but may also employ more common blossoms.

Fresh Flowers Sources

There are three major sources of fresh flowers for retail florists in North America: local growers, local wholesalers and flower auctions.

Miami is considered to be the main distribution point for imported fresh flowers. Many local wholesalers are purchasing fresh flower stock from importers in Miami to resale to local florist in their areas. Wholesale flower districts present in many North American cities such as New York, Boston and San Francisco. Flower auctions are run using Dutch clock system and mainly located in Canada: Toronto, Montreal, and Vancouver. Internationally there are hundreds of wholesale flower markets and auctions, the largest of which is located in Aalsmeer, Holland, the Bloemenveiling Aalsmeer. Other major markets include the fledgling Dubai Flower Centre and the Ota Flower Market in Tokyo, Japan.

Shop Layout

Generally, a florist's shop will contain a large array of flowers, sometimes displayed on the street, or will have a large plate glass window to display the flowers. To keep them fresh, the flowers will be inside of a cooler and kept in water, generally in glass or plastic vases or other containers. Most shops have a cooler near the front of the store with large glass doors so that customers can easily view the contents. Some shops also have another cooler out of the customers' view where they keep extra stock and arrangements for customers' orders. Most stores have a back section in which the designers can work on orders with more privacy.

The vastly divergent views on the colour white can also lead to major flower issues. While white represents death in many Asian cultures, it is simultaneously a symbol of purity and innocence in many European and American cultures. Such differences can lead to difficult issues when a bouquet of white lilies, for example, is delivered.

Supermarket Flowers

Cut flowers are widely sold in supermarkets and gas stations. These outlets offer a limited selection, usually in the form of mixed bouquets and roses by the dozen. Flowers purchased at these outlets are generally less expensive than the same flowers purchased at a florist shop.

Internet Sales

The World Wide Web has had a significant impact on traditional florists, with the North American market experiencing a more than 20 per cent decline in traditional, independently owned flower shops since 1998. Purchases from shops are slowly being overtaken by online flower delivery ordering and floral wire services. However, some independent florists have taken to having their own online store, where customers can order online as well as on the telephone.

2

Flower

A *flower*, sometimes known as a bloom or blossom, is the reproductive structure found in flowering plants (plants of the division Magnoliophyta, also called angiosperms). The biological function of a flower is to mediate the union of male sperm with female ovum in order to produce seeds. The process begins with pollination, is followed by fertilization, leading to the formation and dispersal of the seeds. For the higher plants, seeds are the next generation, and serve as the primary means by which individuals of a species are dispersed across the landscape. The grouping of flowers on a plant is called the inflorescence.

In addition to serving as the reproductive organs of flowering plants, flowers have long been admired and used by humans, mainly to beautify their environment but also as a source of food.

Flowering plants usually face selective pressure to optimise the transfer of their pollen, and this is typically reflected in the morphology of the flowers and the behaviour of the plants. Pollen may be transferred between plants via a number of 'vectors'. Some plants make use of abiotic vectors — namely wind (anemophily) or, much less commonly, *water* (hydrophily). Others use biotic vectors including insects (entomophily), birds (ornithophily), bats (chiropterophily) or other animals. Some plants make use of multiple vectors, but many are highly specialised.

Cleistogamous flowers are self pollinated, after which they may or may not open. Many Viola and some Salvia species are known to have these types of flowers.

The flowers of plants that make use of biotic pollen vectors commonly have glands called nectaries that act as an incentive for animals to visit the flower. Some flowers have patterns, called nectar guides, that show pollinators where to look for nectar. Flowers also attract pollinators by scent and colour. Still other flowers use mimicry to attract pollinators. Some species of orchids, for example, produce flowers resembling female bees in colour, shape, and scent. Flowers are also specialized in shape and have an arrangement of the stamens that ensures that pollen grains are transferred to the bodies of the pollinator when it lands in search of its attractant (such as nectar, pollen, or a mate). In pursuing this attractant from many flowers of the same species, the pollinator transfers pollen to the stigmas — arranged with equally pointed precision — of all of the flowers it visits.

Anemophilous flowers use the wind to move pollen from one flower to the next. Examples include grasses, birch trees, ragweed and maples. They have no need to attract pollinators and therefore tend not to be 'showy' flowers. Male and female reproductive organs are generally found in separate flowers, the male flowers having a number of long filaments terminating in exposed stamens, and the female flowers having long, feather-like stigmas. Whereas the pollen of animal-pollinated flowers tends to be large-grained, sticky, and rich in protein (another 'reward' for pollinators), anemophilous flower pollen is usually small-grained, very light, and of little nutritional value to animals.

Flowering plants are *heterosporangiate,* producing two types of reproductive spores. The pollen (male spores) and ovules (female spores) are produced in different organs, but the typical flower is a *bisporangiate strobilus* in that it contains both organs.

A flower is regarded as a modified stem with shortened internodes and bearing, at its nodes, structures that may be highly modified leaves. In essence, a flower structure forms on a modified shoot or *axis* with an apical meristem that does not grow continuously (growth is *determinate*). Flowers may be attached to the plant in a few ways. If the flower has no stem but forms in the axil of a leaf, it is called 'sessile'. When one flower is produced, the stem holding the flower is called 'a peduncle'. If the peduncle ends with groups of flowers, each stem that holds a flower is called 'a pedicel'. The flowering stem forms a terminal end which is called the *torus* or receptacle. The parts of a flower are arranged in whorls on the torus. The four main parts or whorls (starting from the base of the flower or lowest node and working upwards) are as follows:

- *Calyx*: the outer whorl of *sepals* — typically these are green, but are petal-like in some species.
- *Corolla*: the whorl of *petals*, which are usually thin, soft and coloured to attract animals that help the process of pollination. The colouration may extend into the ultraviolet, which is visible to the compound eyes of insects, but not to the eyes of birds.
- *Androecium* (from Greek *andros oikia*: man's house): one or two whorls of stamens, each a filament topped by an anther where pollen is produced. Pollen contains the male gametes.
- *Gynoecium* (from Greek *gynaikos oikia*: woman's house): one or more pistils. The female reproductive organ is the carpel: this contains an ovary with ovules (which contain female gametes). A pistil may consist of a number of carpels merged together, in which case there is only one pistil to each flower, or of a single individual

carpel (the flower is then called *apocarpous*). The sticky tip of the pistil, the stigma, is the receptor of pollen. The supportive stalk, the style becomes the pathway for pollen tubes to grow from pollen grains adhering to the stigma, to the ovules, carrying the reproductive material.

Although the floral structure described above is considered the 'typical' structural plan, plant species show a wide variety of modifications from this plan. These modifications have significance in the evolution of flowering plants and are used extensively by botanists to establish relationships among plant species. For example, the two subclasses of flowering plants may be distinguished by the number of floral organs in each whorl: dicotyledons typically having 4 or 5 organs (or a multiple of 4 or 5) in each whorl and monocotyledons having three or some multiple of three. The number of carpels in a compound pistil may be only two, or otherwise not related to the above generalization for monocots and dicots.

In the majority of species individual flowers have both pistils and stamens as described above. These flowers are described by botanists as being *perfect, bisexual,* or *hermaphrodite*. However, in some species of plants the flowers are *imperfect* or *unisexual*: having only either male (stamens) or female (pistil) parts. In the latter case, if an individual plant is either female or male the species is regarded as *dioecious*. However, where unisexual male and female flowers appear on the same plant, the species is considered *monoecious*.

Additional discussions on floral modifications from the basic plan are presented in the articles on each of the basic parts of the flower. In those species that have more than one flower on an axis — so-called *composite flowers* — the collection of flowers is termed an *inflorescence;* this term can also refer to the specific arrangements of flowers on a stem. In this regard, care must be exercised in considering what a 'flower' is. In botanical terminology, a single daisy or sunflower for example, is not a flower but a flower *head* — an inflorescence composed of numerous tiny flowers (sometimes called florets). Each of these flowers may be anatomically as described above. Many flowers have a symmetry, if the perianth is bisected through the central axis from any point, symmetrical halves are produced — the flower is called regular or actinomorphic, e.g. rose or trillium. When flowers are bisected and produce only one line that produces symmetrical halves the flower is said to be irregular or zygomorphic. e.g. snapdragon or most orchids.

Floral Formula

A *floral formula* is a way to represent the structure of a flower using specific letters, numbers, and symbols. Typically, a general formula will be used to represent the flower structure of a plant family rather than a particular species. The following representations are used:

Ca = calyx (sepal whorl; e.g. Ca^5 = 5 sepals)

Co = corolla (petal whorl; e. g., $Co^{3(x)}$ = petals some multiple of three)

Z = add if *zygomorphic* (e. g., CoZ^6 = zygomorphic with 6 petals)

A = *androecium* (whorl of stamens; e. g., A^8 = many stamens)

G = *gynoecium* (carpel or carpels; e. g., G^1 = monocarpous)

x : to represent a 'variable number'

8 : to represent 'many'

A floral formula would appear something like this:

$Ca^5Co^5A^{10-8}G^1$

Several additional symbols are sometimes used (see Key to Floral Formulas).

The four main parts of a flower are generally defined by their positions on the receptacle and not by their function. Many flowers lack some parts or parts may be modified into other functions and/or look like what is typically another part. In some families, like Ranunculaceae, the petals are greatly reduced and in many species the sepals are colourful and petal-like. Other flowers have modified stamens that are petal-like, the double flowers of Peonies and Roses are mostly petaloid stamens. Flowers show great variation and plant scientists describe this variation in a systematic way to identify and distinguish species.

Specific terminology is used to descried flowers and their parts. Many flower parts are fused together; fused parts originating from the same whorl are *connate*, while fused parts originating from different whorls are *adnate*, parts that are not fused are *free*. When petals are fused into a tube or ring that falls away as a single unit, they are sympetalous (also called *gamopetalous*). Petals that are connate may have distinctive regions: the cylindrical base is the tube, the expanding region is the throat and the flaring outer region is the limb. A sympetalous flower, with bilateral symmetry with an upper and lower lip, is *bilabiate*. Flowers with connate petals or sepals may have various shaped corolla or calyx including: campanulate, funnelform, tubular, urceolate, salverform or rotate.

Flowering Transition

The transition to flowering is one of the major phase changes that a plant makes during its life cycle. The transition must take place at a time that is favourable for fertilization and the formation of seeds, hence ensuring maximal reproductive success. To meet these needs a plant is able to interpret important endogenous and environmental cues such as changes in levels of plant hormones and seasonable temperature and photoperiod.

Many perennial and most biennial plants require vernalization to flower. The molecular interpretation of these signals is through the transmission of a complex signal known as florigen, which involves a variety of genes, including:

- Constans;
- Flowering locus; and
- Flowering Locus T.

Florigen is produced in the leaves in reproductively favourable conditions and acts in buds and growing tips to induce a number of different physiological and morphological changes. The first step is the transformation of the vegetative stem primordia into floral primordia. This occurs as biochemical changes take place to change cellular differentiation of leaf, bud and stem tissues into tissue that will grow into the reproductive organs. Growth of the central part of the stem tip stops or flattens out and the sides develop protuberances in a whorled or spiral fashion around the outside of the stem end. These protuberances develop into the sepals, petals, stamens, and carpels. Once this process begins, in most plants, it cannot be reversed and the stems develop flowers, even if the initial start of the flower formation event was dependent of some environmental cue. Once the process begins, even if that cue is removed the stem will continue to develop a flower.

Organ Development

The molecular control of floral organ identity determination is fairly well understood. In a simple model, three gene activities interact in a combinatorial manner to determine the developmental identities of the organ primordia within the floral meristem. These gene functions are called *A*, *B* and C-gene functions. In the first floral whorl only *A*-genes are expressed, leading to the formation of sepals. In the second whorl both *A*- and *B*-genes are expressed, leading to the formation of petals. In the third whorl, *B* and *C* genes interact to form stamens and in the center of the flower *C*-genes alone give rise to carpels. The model is based upon studies of homeotic mutants in *Arabidopsis thaliana* and snapdragon, *Antirrhinum majus*. For example, when there is a loss of *B*-gene function, mutant flowers are produced with sepals in the first whorl as usual, but also in the second whorl instead of the normal petal formation. In the third whorl the lack of *B* function but presence of *C*-function mimics the fourth whorl, leading to the formation of carpels also in the third whorl. See also the *ABC* Model of Flower Development.

Most genes central in this model belong to the MADS-box genes and are transcription factors that regulate the expression of the genes specific for each floral organ.

Pollination

The primary purpose of a flower is reproduction. Since the flowers are the reproductive organs of plant, they mediate the joining of the sperm, contained within pollen, to the ovules - contained in the ovary. Pollination is the movement of pollen from the anthers to the stigma. The joining of the sperm to the ovules is called fertilization. Normally pollen is moved from one plant to another, but many plants are able to self pollinate. The fertilized ovules produce seeds that are the next generation. Sexual reproduction produces genetically unique offspring, allowing for adaptation. Flowers have specific designs which encourages the transfer of pollen from one plant to another of the same species. Many plants are dependent upon external factors for pollination, including: wind and animals, and especially insects. Even large animals such as birds, bats, and pygmy possums can be employed. The period of time during which this process can take place (the flower is fully expanded and functional) is called *anthesis*.

Plants can not move from one location to another, thus many flowers have evolved to attract animals to transfer pollen between individuals in dispersed populations. Flowers that are insect-pollinated are called *entomophilous;* literally 'insect-loving' in Latin. They can be highly modified along with the pollinating insects by co-evolution. Flowers commonly have glands called *nectaries* on various parts that attract animals looking for nutritious nectar. Birds and bees have colour vision, enabling them to seek out 'colourful' flowers. Some flowers have patterns, called nectar guides, that show pollinators where to look for nectar; they may be visible only under ultraviolet light, which is visible to bees and some other insects. Flowers also attract pollinators by scent and some of those scents are pleasant to our sense of smell. Not all flower scents are appealing to humans, a number of flowers are pollinated by insects that are attracted to rotten flesh and have flowers that smell like dead animals, often called Carrion flowers including *Rafflesia*, the titan arum, and the North American pawpaw (*Asimina triloba*).

Flowers pollinated by night visitors, including bats and moths, are likely to concentrate on scent to attract pollinators and most such flowers are white.

Still other flowers use mimicry to attract pollinators. Some species of orchids, for example, produce flowers resembling female bees in colour, shape, and scent. Male bees move from one such flower to another in search of a mate.

Pollination Mechanism

Entomophilous: flowers attract and use insects, bats, birds or other animals to transfer pollen from one flower to the next. Often they are specialized in shape and have an arrangement of the stamens that ensures that pollen grains are transferred to the bodies of the pollinator when it lands in search of its attractant (such as nectar, pollen, or a mate). In pursuing this attractant from many flowers of the same species, the pollinator transfers pollen to the stigmas — arranged with equally pointed precision — of all of the flowers it visits. Many flowers rely on simple proximity between flower parts to ensure pollination. Others, such as the *Sarracenia* or lady-slipper orchids, have elaborate designs to ensure pollination while preventing self-pollination.

Anemophilous: flowers use the wind to move pollen from one flower to the next, examples include the grasses, Birch trees, Ragweed and Maples. They have no need to attract pollinators and therefore tend not to be 'showy' flowers. Whereas the pollen of entomophilous flowers tends to be large-grained, sticky, and rich in protein (another 'reward' for pollinators), anemophilous flower pollen is usually small-grained, very light, and of little nutritional value to insects, though it may still be gathered in times of dearth. Honeybees and bumblebees actively gather anemophilous corn (maize) pollen, though it is of little value to them.

Some flowers are self pollinated and use flowers that never open or are self pollinated before the flowers open, these flowers are called cleistogamous. Many Viola species and some Salvia have these types of flowers.

Flower-pollinator Relationships

Many flowers have close relationships with one or a few specific pollinating organisms. Many flowers, for example, attract only one specific species of insect, and therefore rely on that insect for successful reproduction. This close relationship is often given as an example of coevolution, as the flower and pollinator are thought to have developed together over a long period of time to match each other's needs.

This close relationship compounds the negative effects of extinction. The extinction of either member in such a relationship would mean almost certain extinction of the other member as well. Some endangered plant species are so because of shrinking pollinator populations.

Fertilization and Dispersal

Some flowers with both stamens and a pistil are capable of self-fertilization, which does increase the chance of producing seeds but limits genetic variation. The extreme case of self-fertilization occurs in flowers that always self-fertilize, such as many dandelions. Conversely, many species of plants have ways of preventing self-fertilization. Unisexual male and female flowers on the same plant may not appear or mature at the same time, or pollen from the same plant may be incapable of fertilizing its ovules. The latter flower types, which have chemical barriers to their own pollen, are referred to as self-sterile or self-incompatible.

While land plants have existed for about 425 million years, the first ones reproduced by a simple adaptation of their aquatic counterparts: spores. In the sea, plants — and some animals — can simply scatter out genetic clones of themselves to float away and grow elsewhere. This is how early plants reproduced. But plants soon evolved methods of protecting these copies to deal with drying out and other abuse which is even more likely on land than in the sea. The protection became the seed, though it had not yet evolved the flower. Early seed-bearing plants include the ginkgo and conifers. The earliest fossil of a flowering plant, *Archaefructus liaoningensis*, is dated about 125 million years old. Several groups of extinct gymnosperms, particularly seed ferns, have been proposed as the ancestors of flowering plants but there is no continuous fossil evidence showing exactly how flowers evolved. The apparently sudden appearance of relatively modern flowers in the fossil record posed such a problem for the theory of evolution that it was called an 'abominable mystery' by Charles Darwin. Recently discovered angiosperm fossils such as *Archaefructus*, along with further discoveries of fossil gymnosperms, suggest how angiosperm characteristics may have been acquired in a series of steps.

Recent DNA analysis (molecular systematics) shows that *Amborella trichopoda*, found on the Pacific island of New Caledonia, is the sister group to the rest of the flowering plants, and morphological studies suggest that it has features which may have been characteristic of the earliest flowering plants.

The general assumption is that the function of flowers, from the start, was to involve other animals in the reproduction process. Pollen can be scattered without bright colours and obvious shapes, which would therefore be a liability, using the plant's resources, unless they provide some other benefit. One proposed reason for the sudden, fully developed appearance of flowers is that they evolved in an isolated setting like an island, or chain of islands, where the plants bearing them were able to develop a highly specialized relationship with some specific animal (a wasp, for example), the way many island species develop today. This symbiotic relationship, with a hypothetical wasp bearing pollen from one plant to another much the way fig wasps do today, could have eventually resulted in both the plant(s) and their partners developing a high degree of specialization. Island genetics is believed to be a common source of speciation, especially when it comes to radical adaptations which seem to have required inferior transitional forms. Note that the wasp example is not incidental; bees, apparently evolved specifically for symbiotic plant relationships, are descended from wasps.

Likewise, most fruit used in plant reproduction comes from the enlargement of parts of the flower. This fruit is frequently a tool which depends upon animals wishing to eat it, and thus scattering the seeds it contains.

While many such symbiotic relationships remain too fragile to survive competition with mainland animals and spread, flowers proved to be an unusually effective means of production, spreading (whatever their actual origin) to become the dominant form of land plant life.

While there is only hard proof of such flowers existing about 130 million years ago, there is some circumstantial evidence that they did exist up to 250 million years ago. A chemical used by plants to defend their flowers, oleanane, has been detected in fossil plants that old, including gigantopterids, which evolved at that time and bear many of the traits of modern, flowering plants, though they are not known to be flowering plants themselves, because only their stems and prickles have been found preserved in detail; one of the earliest examples of petrification.

The similarity in leaf and stem structure can be very important, because flowers are genetically just an adaptation of normal leaf and stem components on plants, a combination of genes normally responsible for forming new shoots. The most primitive flowers are thought to have had a variable number of flower parts, often separate from (but in contact with) each other. The flowers would have tended to grow in a spiral pattern, to be bisexual (in plants, this means both male and female parts on the same flower), and to be dominated by the ovary (female part). As flowers grew more advanced, some variations developed parts fused together, with a much more specific number and design, and with either specific sexes per flower or plant, or at least 'ovary inferior'.

Flower evolution continues to the present day—modern flowers have been so profoundly influenced by humans that many of them cannot be pollinated in nature. Many modern, domesticated flowers used to be simple weeds, which only sprouted when the ground was disturbed. Some of them tended to grow with human crops, and the prettiest did not get plucked because of their beauty, developing a dependence upon and special adaptation to human affection.

Many flowers have important symbolic meanings in Western culture. The practice of assigning meanings to flowers is known as floriography. Some of the more common examples include:

- Passion

Poppies are a symbol of consolation in time of death. In the UK, New Zealand, Australia and Canada, red poppies are worn to commemorate soldiers who have died in times of war.

Irises/Lily are used in burials as a symbol referring to 'resurrection/life'. It is also associated with stars (sun) and its petals blooming/shining.

Daisies are a symbol of innocence.

Flowers within art are also representative of the female genitalia, as seen in the works of artists such as Georgia O'Keeffe, Imogen Cunningham, Veronica Ruiz de Velasco, and Judy Chicago, and in fact in Asian and western classical art. Many cultures around the world have a marked tendency to associate flowers with femininity.

The great variety of delicate and beautiful flowers has inspired the works of numerous poets, especially from the 18th-19th century Romantic era. Famous examples include William Wordsworth's *I Wandered Lonely as a Cloud* and William Blake's *Ah! Sun-Flower*.

Because of their varied and colourful appearance, flowers have long been a favourite subject of visual artists as well. Some of the most celebrated paintings from well-known painters are of flowers, such as Van Gogh's sunflowers series or Monet's water lilies. Flowers are also dried, freeze dried and pressed in order to create permanent, three-dimensional pieces of flower art.

The Roman goddess of flowers, gardens, and the season of Spring is Flora. The Greek goddess of spring, flowers and nature is Chloris.

In Hindu mythology, flowers have a significant status. Vishnu, one of the three major gods in the Hindu system, is often depicted standing straight on a lotus flower. Apart from the association with Vishnu, the Hindu tradition also considers the lotus to have spiritual significance. For example, it figures in the Hindu stories of creation.

In modern times, people have sought ways to cultivate, buy, wear, or otherwise be around flowers and blooming plants, partly because of their agreeable appearance and smell. Around the world, people use flowers for a wide range of events and functions that, cumulatively, encompass one's lifetime:

- For new births or christenings.
- As a corsage or boutonniere to be worn at social functions or for holidays.
- As tokens of love or esteem.
- For wedding flowers for the bridal party, and decorations for the hall.
- As brightening decorations within the home.
- As a gift of remembrance for bon voyage parties, welcome home parties, and 'thinking of you' gifts.
- For funeral flowers and expressions of sympathy for the grieving.
- For worshiping goddesses. in Hindu culture it is very common to bring flowers as a gift to temples.

People therefore grow flowers around their homes, dedicate entire parts of their living space to flower gardens, pick wildflowers, or buy flowers from florists who depend on an entire network of commercial growers and shippers to support their trade.

Flowers provide less food than other major plants parts (seeds, fruits, roots, stems and leaves) but they provide several important foods and spices. Flower vegetables include broccoli, cauliflower and artichoke. The most expensive spice, saffron, consists of dried stigmas of a crocus. Other flower spices are cloves and capers.

Hops flowers are used to flavour beer. Marigold flowers are fed to chickens to give their egg yolks a golden yellow colour, which consumers find more desirable. Dandelion flowers are often made into wine. Bee Pollen, pollen collected from bees, is considered a health food by some people. Honey consists of bee-processed flower nectar and is often named for the type of flower, e.g. orange blossom honey, clover honey and tupelo honey.

Hundreds of fresh flowers are edible but few are widely marketed as food. They are often used to add colour and flavour to salads. Squash flowers are dipped in breadcrumbs and fried. Edible flowers include nasturtium, chrysanthemum, carnation, cattail, honeysuckle, chicory, cornflower, canna, and sunflower. Some edible flowers are sometimes candied such as daisy and rose (you may also come across a candied pansy).

Flowers can also be made into herbal teas. Dried flowers such as chrysanthemum, rose, jasmine, camomile are infused into tea both for their fragrance and medical properties. Sometimes, they are also mixed with tea leaves for the added fragrance.

3

Flowering Plant

The *flowering plants* or *angiosperms* (*Angiospermae* or *Magnoliophyta*) are the most diverse group of land plants. The flowering plants and the gymnosperms are the only extant groups of seed plants. The flowering plants are distinguished from other seed plants by a series of apomorphies, or derived characteristics.

The ancestors of flowering plants diverged from gymnosperms around 245-202 million years ago, and the first flowering plants known to exist are from 140 million years ago. They diversified enormously during the Lower Cretaceous and became widespread around 100 million years ago, but replaced conifers as the dominant trees only around 60-100 million years ago.

The flowers, which are the reproductive organs of flowering plants, are the most remarkable feature distinguishing them from other seed plants. Flowers aid angiosperms by enabling a wider range of adaptability and broadening the ecological niches open to them. This has allowed flowering plants to largely dominate terrestrial ecosystems.

Stamens with Two Pairs of Pollen Sacs

Stamens are much lighter than the corresponding organs of gymnosperms and have contributed to the diversification of angiosperms through time with adaptations to specialized pollination syndromes, such as particular pollinators. Stamens have also become modified through time to prevent self-fertilization, which has permitted further diversification, allowing angiosperms eventually to fill more niches.

The male gametophyte in angiosperms is significantly reduced in size compared to those of gymnosperm seed plants. The smaller pollen decreases the time from pollination — the pollen grain reaching the female plant — to fertilization of the ovary; in gymnosperms fertilization can occur up to a year after pollination, while in angiosperms the fertilization begins very soon after pollination. The shorter time leads to angiosperm plants setting seeds sooner and faster than gymnosperms, which is a distinct evolutionary advantage.

The closed carpel of angiosperms also allows adaptations to specialized pollination syndromes and controls. This helps to prevent self-fertilization, thereby maintaining increased diversity. Once the ovary is fertilized, the carpel and some surrounding tissues develop into a fruit. This fruit often serves as an attractant to seed-dispersing animals. The resulting cooperative relationship presents another advantage to angiosperms in the process of dispersal.

The reduced female gametophyte, like the reduced male gametophyte, may be an adaptation allowing for more rapid seed set, eventually leading to such flowering plant adaptations as annual herbaceous life cycles, allowing the flowering plants to fill even more niches.

Endosperm formation generally begins after fertilization and before the first division of the zygote. Endosperm is a highly nutritive tissue that can provide food for the developing embryo, the cotyledons, and sometimes for the seedling when it first appears.

These distinguishing characteristics taken together have made the angiosperms the most diverse and numerous land plants and the most commercially important group to humans. The major exception to the dominance of terrestrial ecosystems by flowering plants is the coniferous forest.

Evolution

Land plants have existed for about 425 million years. Early land plants reproduced sexually with flagellated, swimming sperm, like the green algae from which they evolved. An adaptation to terrestrialization was the development of upright meiosporangia for dispersal by spores to new habitats. This feature is lacking in the descendants of their nearest algal relatives, the Charophycean green algae. A later terrestrial adaptation took place with retention of the delicate, avascular sexual stage, the gametophyte, within the tissues of the vascular sporophyte. This occurred by spore germination within sporangia rather than spore release, as in non-seed plants. A current example of how this might have happened can be seen in the precocious spore germination in *Sellaginella*, the spike-moss. The result for the ancestors of angiosperms was enclosing them in a case, the seed. The first seed bearing plants, like the ginkgo, and conifers (such as pines and firs), did not produce flowers. Interestingly, the pollen grains (males) of *Ginkgo* and cycads produce a pair of flagellated, mobile sperm cells that 'swim' down the developing pollen tube to the female and her eggs.

The apparently sudden appearance of relatively modern flowers in the fossil record posed such a problem for the theory of evolution that it was called an *'abominable mystery'* by Charles Darwin. However, the fossil record has grown since the time of Darwin, and recently discovered angiosperm fossils such as *Archaefructus*, along with further discoveries of fossil gymnosperms, suggest how angiosperm characteristics may have been acquired in a series of steps. Several groups of extinct gymnosperms, particularly seed ferns, have been proposed as the ancestors of flowering plants but there is no continuous fossil evidence showing exactly how flowers evolved. Some older fossils, such as the upper Triassic *Sanmiguelia*, have been suggested. Based on current evidence, some propose that the ancestors of the angiosperms diverged from an unknown group of gymnosperms during the late Triassic (245-202 million years ago). A close relationship between angiosperms and gnetophytes, proposed on the basis of morphological evidence, has more recently been disputed on the basis of molecular evidence that suggest gnetophytes are instead more closely related to other gymnosperms.

The earliest known macrofossil confidently identified as an angiosperm, *Archaefructus liaoningensis*, is dated to about 125 million years BP (the Cretaceous period), while pollen considered to be of angiosperm origin takes the fossil record back to about 130 million years BP. However, one study has suggested that the early-middle Jurassic plant *Schmeissneria*, traditionally considered a type of ginkgo, may be the earliest known angiosperm, or at least a close relative. Additionally, circumstantial chemical evidence for the existence of angiosperms as early as 250 million years ago. Oleanane, a secondary metabolite produced by many flowering plants, has been found in Permian deposits of that age together with fossils of gigantopterids. Gigantopterids are a group of extinct seed plants that share many morphological traits with flowering plants, although they are not known to have been flowering plants themselves.

Recent DNA analysis (molecular systematics) show that *Amborella trichopoda*, found on the Pacific island of New Caledonia, belongs to a sister group of the other flowering plants, and morphological studies suggest that it has features that may have been characteristic of the earliest flowering plants.

The great angiosperm radiation, when a great diversity of angiosperms appears in the fossil record, occurred in the mid-Cretaceous (approximately 100 million years ago). However, a study in 2007 estimated that the division of the five most recent (the genus *Ceratophyllum*, the family Chloranthaceae, the eudicots, the magnoliids, and the monocots) of the eight main groups occurred around 140 million years ago. By the late Cretaceous, angiosperms appear to have dominated environments formerly occupied by ferns and cycadophytes, but large canopy-forming trees replaced conifers as the dominant trees only close to the end of the Cretaceous 65 millions years ago or even later, at the beginning of the Tertiary. The radiation of herbaceous angiosperm occurred much later. Yet, many fossil plants recognizable as belonging to modern families (including beech, oak, maple, and magnolia) appeared already at late Cretaceous.

It is generally assumed that the function of flowers, from the start, was to involve mobile animals in their reproduction processes. That is, pollen can be scattered even if the flower is not brightly coloured or oddly shaped in a way that attracts animals; however, by expending the energy required to create such traits, angiosperms can enlist the aid of animals and thus reproduce more efficiently.

Island genetics provides one proposed explanation for the sudden, fully developed appearance of flowering plants. Island genetics is believed to be a common source of speciation in general, especially when it comes to radical adaptations that seem to have required inferior transitional forms. Flowering plants may have evolved in an isolated setting like an island or island chain, where the plants bearing them were able to develop a highly specialized relationship with some specific animal (a wasp, for example). Such a relationship, with a hypothetical wasp carrying pollen from one plant to another much the way fig wasps do today, could result in both the plant(s) and their partners developing a high degree of specialization. Note that the wasp example is not incidental; bees, which apparently evolved specifically due to mutualistic plant relationships, are descended from wasps.

Animals are also involved in the distribution of seeds. Fruit, which is formed by the enlargement of flower parts, is frequently a seed-dispersal tool that attracts animals to eat or otherwise disturb it, incidentally scattering the seeds it contains. While many such mutualistic relationships remain too fragile to survive competition and spread widely, flowering proved to be an unusually effective means of reproduction, spreading (whatever its origin) to become the dominant form of land plant life.

Flower ontogeny uses a combination of genes normally responsible for forming new shoots. The most primitive flowers are thought to have had a variable number of flower parts, often separate from (but in contact with) each other. The flowers would have tended to grow in a spiral pattern, to be bisexual (in plants, this means both male and female parts on the same flower), and to be dominated by the ovary (female part). As flowers grew more advanced, some variations developed parts fused together, with a much more specific number and design, and with either specific sexes per flower or plant, or at least 'ovary inferior'.

Flower evolution continues to the present day; modern flowers have been so profoundly influenced by humans that some of them cannot be pollinated in nature. Many modern, domesticated flowers used to be simple weeds, which only sprouted when the ground was disturbed. Some of them tended to grow with human crops, perhaps already having symbiotic companion plant relationships with them, and the prettiest did not get plucked because of their beauty, developing a dependence upon and special adaptation to human affection.

There are eight groups of living angiosperms:

- *Amborella*— a single species of shrub from New Caledonia.
- *Nymphaeales*— about 80 species water lilies and Hydatellaceae.

- *Austrobaileyales*— about 100 species of woody plants from various parts of the world.
- *Chloranthales*— several dozen species of aromatic plants with toothed leaves.
- *Magnoliidae*— about 9,000 species, characterized by trimerous flowers, pollen with one pore, and usually branching-veined leaves — for example magnolias, bay laurel, and black pepper.
- *Monocotyledonae*— about 70,000 species, characterized by trimerous flowers, a single cotyledon, pollen with one pore, and usually parallel-veined leaves – for example grasses, orchids, and palms.
- *Ceratophyllum*— about 6 species of aquatic plants, perhaps most familiar as aquarium plants.
- *Eudicotyledonae*— about 1,75,000 species, characterized by 4 or 5 merous flowers, pollen with three pores, and usually branching-veined leaves — for example sunflowers, petunia, buttercup, apples and oaks.

The exact relationship between these eight groups is not yet clear, although it has been determined that the first three groups to diverge from the ancestral angiosperm were Amborellales, Nymphaeales, and Austrobaileyales. The term basal angiosperms refers to these three groups. The five other groups form the clade Mesangiospermae, with the Chloranthales and Magnoliidae forming the basal mesangiosperms. *Ceratophyllum* seems to group with the eudicots rather than with the monocots.

The botanical term 'Angiosperm', from the Ancient Greek, *angeíon* (receptacle, vessel) and (seed), was coined in the form Angiospermae by Paul Hermann in 1690, as the name of that one of his primary divisions of the plant kingdom. This included flowering plants possessing seeds enclosed in capsules, distinguished from his Gymnospermae, or flowering plants with achenial or schizo-carpic fruits, the whole fruit or each of its pieces being here regarded as a seed and naked. The term and its antonym were maintained by Carolus Linnaeus with the same sense, but with restricted application, in the names of the orders of his class Didynamia. Its use with any approach to its modern scope only became possible after 1827, when Robert Brown established the existence of truly naked ovules in the Cycadeae and Coniferae, and applied to them the name Gymnosperms. From that time onwards, so long as these Gymnosperms were, as was usual, reckoned as dicotyledonous flowering plants, the term Angiosperm was used antithetically by botanical writers, with varying scope, as a group-name for other dicotyledonous plants.

In 1851, Hofmeister discovered the changes occurring in the embryo-sac of flowering plants, and determined the correct relationships of these to the Cryptogamia. This fixed the position of Gymnosperms as a class distinct from Dicotyledons, and the term Angiosperm then gradually came to be accepted as the suitable designation for the whole of the flowering plants other than Gymnosperms, including the classes of Dicotyledons and Monocotyledons. This is the sense in which the term is used today.

In most taxonomies, the flowering plants are treated as a coherent group. The most popular descriptive name has been Angiospermae (Angiosperms), with Anthophyta ('flowering plants') a second choice. These names are not linked to any rank. The Wettstein system and the Engler system use the name Angiospermae, at the assigned rank of subdivision. The Reveal system treated flowering plants as subdivision Magnoliophytina, but later split it to Magnoliopsida, Liliopsida and Rosopsida. The Takhtajan system and Cronquist system treat this group at the rank of division, leading to the name Magnoliophyta (from the family name Magnoliaceae). The Dahlgren system and Thorne system (1992) treat this group at the rank of class, leading to the name Magnoliopsida. However, the APG system, of

1998, and the APG II system, of 2003 , do not treat it as a formal taxon but rather treat it as a clade without a formal botanical name and use the name angiosperms for this clade.

The internal classification of this group has undergone considerable revision. The Cronquist system, proposed by Arthur Cronquist in 1968 and published in its full form in 1981, is still widely used, but is no longer believed to accurately reflect phylogeny. A general consensus about how the flowering plants should be arranged has recently begun to emerge, through the work of the Angiosperm Phylogeny Group, who published an influential reclassification of the angiosperms in 1998. An update incorporating more recent research was published as APG II in 2003.

Traditionally, the flowering plants are divided into two groups, which in the Cronquist system are called *Magnoliopsida* (at the rank of class, formed from the family name *Magnoliacae*) and *Liliopsida* (at the rank of class, formed from the family name *Liliaceae*). Other descriptive names allowed by Article 16 of the ICBN include *Dicotyledones* or *Dicotyledoneae,* and *Monocotyledones* or *Monocotyledoneae,* which have a long history of use. In English a member of either group may be called a *dicotyledon* (plural *dicotyledons*) and *monocotyledon* (plural *monocotyledons*), or abbreviated, as *dicot* (plural *dicots*) and *monocot* (plural *monocots*). These names derive from the observation that the dicots most often have two *cotyledons*, or embryonic leaves, within each seed. The monocots usually have only one, but the rule is not absolute either way. From a diagnostic point of view the number of cotyledons is neither a particularly handy nor reliable character.

Recent studies, as by the APG, show that the monocots form holophyletic or monophyletic group; this clade is given the name *monocots*. However, the dicots are not (they are a paraphyletic group). Nevertheless, within the dicots a monophyletic group does exist, called the *eudicots* or *tricolpates*, and including most of the dicots. The name *tricolpates* derives from a type of pollen found widely within this group. The name *eudicots* is formed combining *dicot* with the prefix *eu-* (from Greek, for 'well,' or 'good,' botanically indicating 'true'), as the eudicots share the characters traditionally attributed to the dicots, such as flowers with four or five parts (four or five petals, four or five sepals). Separating this group of eudicots from the rest of the (former) dicots leaves a remainder, which sometimes are called informally *palaeodicots* (Greek prefix *'palaeo-'* means 'old'). As this remnant group is not monophyletic this is a term of convenience only.

The number of species of flowering plants is estimated to be in the range of 250,000 to 400,000. The number of families in APG (1998) was 462. In APG II (2003) it is not settled; at maximum it is 457, but within this number there are 55 optional segregates, so that the minimum number of families in this system is 402.

The diversity of flowering plants is not evenly distributed. Nearly all species belong to the eudicot (75%), monocot (23%) and magnoliid (2%) clades. The remaining 5 clades contain a little over 250 species in total, i.e., less than 0.1 per cent of flowering plant diversity, divided among 9 families.

The most diverse families of flowering plants, in their APG circumscriptions, in order of number of species, are:

- Asteraceae or Compositae (daisy family): 23,600 species
- Orchidaceae (orchid family): 22,075 species
- Fabaceae or Leguminosae (pea family): 19,400
- Rubiaceae (madder family): 13,150
- Poaceae or Gramineae (grass family): 10,035
- Lamiaceae or Labiatae (mint family): 7,173
- Euphorbiaceae (spurge family): 5,735
- Melastomataceae (melastome family): 5,005

- Myrtaceae (myrtle family): 4,620
- Apocynaceae (dogbane family): 4,555

In the list above (showing only the 10 largest families), the Orchidaceae and Poaceae are monocot families; the others are eudicot families.

The amount and complexity of tissue-formation in flowering plants exceeds that of Gymnosperms. The vascular bundles of the stem are arranged such that the xylem and phloem form concentric rings.

In the Dicotyledons, the bundles in the very young stem are arranged in an open ring, separating a central pith from an outer cortex. In each bundle, separating the xylem and phloem, is a layer of meristem or active formative tissue known as cambium. By the formation of a layer of cambium between the bundles (interfascicular cambium) a complete ring is formed, and a regular periodical increase in thickness results from the development of xylem on the inside and phloem on the outside. The soft phloem becomes crushed, but the hard wood persists and forms the bulk of the stem and branches of the woody perennial. Owing to differences in the character of the elements produced at the beginning and end of the season, the wood is marked out in transverse section into concentric rings, one for each season of growth, called annual rings.Among the Monocotyledons, the bundles are more numerous in the young stem and are scattered through the ground tissue. They contain no cambium and once formed the stem increases in diameter only in exceptional cases.

The characteristic feature of angiosperms is the flower. Flowers show remarkable variation in form and elaboration, and provide the most trustworthy external characteristics for establishing relationships among angiosperm species. The function of the flower is to ensure fertilization of the ovule and development of fruit containing seeds. The floral apparatus may arise terminally on a shoot or from the axil of a leaf (where the petiole attaches to the stem). Occasionally, as in violets, a flower arises singly in the axil of an ordinary foliage-leaf. More typically, the flower-bearing portion of the plant is sharply distinguished from the foliage-bearing or vegetative portion, and forms a more or less elaborate branch-system called an inflorescence.

The reproductive cells produced by flowers are of two kinds. Microspores, which will divide to become pollen grains, are the 'male' cells and are borne in the stamens (or microsporophylls). The 'female' cells called megaspores, which will divide to become the egg-cell (megagametogenesis), are contained in the ovule and enclosed in the carpel (or megasporophyll).

The flower may consist only of these parts, as in willow, where each flower comprises only a few stamens or two carpels. Usually other structures are present and serve to protect the sporophylls and to form an envelope attractive to pollinators. The individual members of these surrounding structures are known as sepals and petals (or tepals in flowers such as *Magnolia* where sepals and petals are not distinguishable from each other). The outer series (calyx of sepals) is usually green and leaf-like, and functions to protect the rest of the flower, especially the bud. The inner series (corolla of petals) is generally white or brightly coloured, and is more delicate in structure. It functions to attract insect or bird pollinators. Attraction is effected by colour, scent, and nectar, which may be secreted in some part of the flower. The characteristics that attract pollinators account for the popularity of flowers and flowering plants among humans.

While the majority of flowers are perfect or hermaphrodite (having both male and female parts in the same flower structure), flowering plants have developed numerous morphological and physiological mechanisms to reduce or prevent self-fertilization. Heteromorphic flowers have short carpels and long stamens, or vice versa, so animal pollinators cannot easily transfer pollen to the pistil (receptive part of the carpel). Homomorphic flowers may employ a biochemical (physiological) mechanism called self-incompatibility to discriminate between self- and non-self pollen grains. In other species, the male and female parts are morphologically separated, developing on different flowers.

Double fertilization refers to a process in which two sperm cells fertilize cells in the ovary. This process begins when a pollen grain adheres to the stigma of the pistil (female reproductive structure), germinates, and grows a long pollen tube. While this pollen tube is growing, a haploid generative cell travels down the tube behind the tube nucleus. The generative cell divides by mitosis to produce two haploid (n) sperm cells. As the pollen tube grows, it makes its way from the stigma, down the style and into the ovary. Here the pollen tube reaches the micropyle of the ovule and digests its way into one of the synergids, releasing its contents (which include the sperm cells). The synergid that the cells were released into degenerates and one sperm makes its way to fertilize the egg cell, producing a diploid ($2n$) zygote. The second sperm cell fuses with both central cell nuclei, producing a triploid ($3n$) cell. As the zygote develops into an embryo, the triploid cell develops into the endosperm, which serves as the embryo's food supply. The ovary now will develop into fruit and the ovule will develop into seed.

As the development of embryo and endosperm proceeds within the embryo-sac, the sac wall enlarges and combines with the nucellus (which is likewise enlarging) and the integument to form the *seed-coat*. The ovary wall develops to form the fruit or pericarp, whose form is closely associated with the manner of distribution of the seed.

Frequently the influence of fertilization is felt beyond the ovary, and other parts of the flower take part in the formation of the fruit, *e.g.* the floral receptacle in the apple, strawberry and others.

The character of the seed-coat bears a definite relation to that of the fruit. They protect the embryo and aid in dissemination; they may also directly promote germination. Among plants with indehiscent fruits, the fruit generally provides protection for the embryo and secures dissemination. In this case, the seed-coat is only slightly developed. If the fruit is dehiscent and the seed is exposed, the seed-coat is generally well developed, and must discharge the functions otherwise executed by the fruit.

Economic Importance

Agriculture is almost entirely dependent on angiosperms, either directly or indirectly through livestock feed. Of all the families plants, the Poaceae, or grass family, is by far the most important, providing the bulk of all feedstocks (rice, corn — maize, wheat, barley, rye, oats, pearl millet, sugar cane, sorghum). The Fabaceae, or legume family, comes in second place. Also of high importance are the Solanaceae, or nightshade family (potatoes, tomatoes, and peppers, among others), the Cucurbitaceae, or gourd family (also including pumpkins and melons), the Brassicaceae, or mustard plant family (including rapeseed and cabbage), and the Apiaceae, or parsley family. Many of our fruits come from the Rutaceae, or rue family, and the Rosaceae, or rose family (including apples, pears, cherries, apricots, plums, etc.).

In some parts of the world, certain single species assume paramount importance because of their variety of uses, for example the coconut (*Cocos nucifera*) on Pacific atolls, and the olive (*Olea europaea*) in the Mediterranean region.

Flowering plants also provide economic resources in the form of wood, paper, fiber (cotton, flax, and hemp, among others), medicines (digitalis, camphor), decorative and landscaping plants, and many other uses. The main area in which they are surpassed by other plants is timber production.

4

Inflorescence

An *inflorescence* is a group or cluster of flowers arranged on a stem that is composed of a main branch or a complicated arrangement of branches. Strictly, it is the part of the shoot of seed plants where flowers are formed and which is accordingly modified. The modifications can involve the length and the nature of the internodes and the phyllotaxis, as well as variations in the proportions, compressions, swellings, adnations, connations and reduction of main and secondary axes.

The stem holding the whole inflorescence is called a *peduncle* and the main stem holding the flowers or more branches within the inflorescence is called the *rachis*. The stalk of each single flower is called a *pedicel*.

The fruiting stage of an inflorescence is known as an infructescence.

A flower that is not part of an inflorescence is called a solitary flower and its stalk is also referred to as a peduncle.

General Characteristics

Inflorescences are described by many different characteristics including how the flowers are arranged on the peduncle, the blooming order of the flowers and how different clusters of flowers are grouped within it. These terms are general representations as plants in nature can have a combination of types.

Bracts

Inflorescences usually have modified foliage different from the vegetative part of the plant. Considering the broadest meaning of the term, any leaf associated with an inflorescence is called a ***bract***. A bract is usually located at the node where the main stem of the inflorescence forms, joined to the main stem of the plant, but other bracts can exist within the inflorescence itself. They serve a variety of functions which include attracting pollinators and protecting young flowers. According to the presence or absence of bracts and their characteristics we can distinguish:

- ***Ebracteate inflorescences:*** No bracts in the inflorescence.
- ***Bracteate inflorescences:*** The bracts in the inflorescence are very specialised, sometimes reduced to small scales, divided or dissected.
- ***Leafy inflorescences:*** Though often reduced in size, the bracts are unspecialised and look like the typical leaves of the plant, so that the term flowering stem is usually applied instead of inflorescence. This use is not technically correct, as, despite their 'normal' appearance, these *leaves* are considered, in fact, *bracts*, so that 'leafy inflorescence' is preferable.
- ***Leafy-bracted inflorescences:*** Intermediate between bracteate and leafy inflorescence.

If many bracts are present and they are strictly connected to the stem, like in the family Asteraceae, the bracts might collectively be called an *involucre*. If the inflorescence has a second unit of bracts further up the stem, they might be called an involucel.

Terminal Flower

Plant organs can grow according to two different schemes, namely monopodial and sympodial. In inflorescences these two different growth patterns are called indeterminate or determinate, and indicate whether a terminal flower is formed and where flowering starts within the inflorescence.

Indeterminate inflorescence: Monopodial growth. The terminal bud keeps growing and forming lateral flowers. A terminal flower is never formed.

Determinate inflorescence: Sympodial growth. The terminal bud forms a terminal flower and then dies out. Other flowers then grow from lateral buds.

Indeterminate and determinate inflorescences are sometimes referred to as open and closed inflorescences respectively.

In *determinate inflorescences* the terminal flower is usually the first to mature (precursive development), while the others tend to mature starting from the bottom of the stem. This pattern is called *acropetal* maturation. When flowers start to mature from the top of the stem, maturation is *basipetal*, while when the central mature first, *divergent*.

In *indeterminate inflorescence* there is no true terminal flower and the stem usually has a rudimentary end. In many cases the last true flower formed by the terminal bud (*subterminal* flower) straightens up, appearing to be a terminal flower. Often a vestige of the terminal bud may be noticed higher on the stem.

Phyllotaxis

As with leaves, flowers can be arranged on the stem according to many different patterns. See 'Phyllotaxis' for in-depth descriptions

Metatopy

Metatopy is the placement of organs out of their normally expected position: typically metatopy occurs in inflorescences when unequal growth rates alter different areas of the axis and the organs attached to the axis.

When a single or a cluster of flower(s) is located at the axil of a bract, the location of the bract in relation to the stem holding the flower(s) is indicated by the use of different terms and may be a useful diagnostic indicator.

Typical placement of bracts include:

- Some plants have bracts that subtend the inflorescence, where the flowers are on branched stalks; the bracts are not connected to the stalks holding the flowers, but are adnate or attached to the main stem (Adnate describes the fusing together of different unrelated parts. When the parts fused together are the same, they are connately joined).
- Other plants have the bracts subtend the pedicel or peduncle of single flowers.

Metatopic placement of bracts include:

- When the bract is attached to the stem holding the flower (the pedicel or peduncle), it is said to be *recaulescent*; sometimes these bracts or bracteoles are highly modified and appear to be appendages of the flower calyx. Recaulescences is the fusion of the subtending leaf with the stem holding the bud or the bud itself, thus the leaf or bract is adnate to the stem of flower.
- When the formation of the bud is shifted up the stem distinctly above the subtending leaf, it is described as *concaulescent*.

There is no general consensus in defining the different inflorescences. The following is based on Focko Weberling's *Morphologie der Blüten und der Blütenstände*.

The main groups of inflorescences are distinguished by branching. Within these groups, the most important characteristics are the intersection of the axes and different variations of the model.

Inflorescences can be *simple* or *compound*.

Simple Inflorescences

Indeterminate

Indeterminate simple inflorescences are generally called *racemose*. The main kind of racemose inflorescence is the *raceme* (pronounced 'raseem', from classical Latin *racemus*, cluster of grapes). The other kind of racemose inflorescences can all be derived from this one by dilation, compression, swelling or reduction of the different axes. Some passage forms between the obvious ones are commonly admitted.

A *raceme* is an unbranched, ndeterminate inflorescence with pedicellate (having short floral stalks) flowers along the axis.

A *spike* is a type of raceme with flowers that do not have a pedicel.

A racemose *corymb* is an unbranched, indeterminate inflorescence that is flat-topped or convex due to their outer pedicels which are progressively longer than inner ones.

An *umbel* is a type of raceme with a short axis and multiple floral pedicels of equal length that appear to arise from a common point.

A *spadix* is a spike of flowers densely arranged around it, enclosed or accompanied by a highly specialised bract called a spathe. It is characteristic of the Araceae family.

A *flower head* or *capitulum* is a very contracted raceme in which the single sessile flowers share are borne on an enlarged stem. It is characteristic of dipsacaceae.

A *catkin* or *ament* is a scaly, generally drooping spike or raceme. Cymose or other complex inflorescences that are superficially similar are also generally called thus.

Determinate

Determinate simple inflorescences are generally called cymose. The main kind of cymose inflorescence is the cyme (pronounced 'saim', from the French *cime* in the sense 'top, summit'). Cymes are further divided according to this scheme:

- Only one secondary axis: *monochasium*
- Secondary buds always develop on the same side of the stem: *helicoid* cyme or *bostryx*
- The successive pedicels are aligned on the same plane: *drepanium*
- Secondary buds develop alternately on the stem: *scorpioid cyme*
- The successive pedicels are arranged in a sort of spiral: *cincinnus* (characteristic of the Boraginaceae and Commelinaceae)
- The successive pedicels follow a zig-zag path on the same plane: *rhipidium* (many Iridaceae)
- Two secondary axes: *dichasial cyme*
- Secondary axis still dichasial: *dichasium* (characteristic of Caryophyllaceae)
- Secondary axis monochasia: *double scorpioid* cyme or *double helicoid* cyme
- More than two secondary axes: *pleiochasium*

A cyme can also be so compressed that it looks like an umbel. Strictly speaking this kind of inflorescence could be called *umbelliform cyme,* although it is normally called simply 'umbel'.

Another kind of definite simple inflorescence is the raceme-like cyme or *botryoid;* that is as a raceme with a terminal flower and is usually.

A reduced raceme or cyme that grows in the axil of a bract is called a *fascicle.* A *verticillaster* is a fascicle with the structure of a dichasium; it is common among the Lamiaceae. Many verticillasters with reduced bracts can form a spicate (spike-like) inflorescence that is commonly called a *spike.*

Compound Inflorescences

Simple inflorescences are the basis for compound inflorescences or *synflorescences*. The single flowers are there replaced by a simple inflorescence, which can be both a racemose or a cymose one. Compound inflorescences are composed of branched stems and can involve complicated arrangements that are difficult to trace back to the main branch.

A kind of compound inflorescence is the double inflorescence, in which the basic structure is repeated in the place of single florets. For example a double raceme is a raceme in which the single flowers are replaced by other simple racemes; the same structure can be repeated to form triple or more complex structures.

Compound raceme inflorescences can either end with a final raceme (*homoeothetic*), or not (*heterothetic*). A compound raceme is often called a *panicle*. Note that this definition is very different from that given by Weberling.

Compound umbels are umbels in which the single flowers are replaced by many smaller umbels called *umbellets*. The stem attaching the side umbellets to the main stem is called a *ray*.

The most common kind of definite compound inflorescence is the *panicle* (of Webeling, or 'panicle-like cyme'). A panicle is a definite inflorescence that is increasingly more strongly and irregularly branched from the top to the bottom and where each branching has a terminal flower.

The so called cymose *corymb* is similar to a racemose corymb but has a panicle-like structure. Another type of panicle is the *anthela*. An anthela is a cymose corymb with the lateral flowers higher than the central ones.

A raceme in which the single flowers are replaced by cymes is called a (indefinite) *thyrse*. The secondary cymes can of course be of any of the different types of dichasia and monochasia. A botryoid in which the single flowers are replaced by cymes is a *definite thyrse* or *thyrsoid*. Thyrses are often confusingly called panicles.

The family Asteraceae is characterised by a highly specialised head technically called a *calathid* (but usually referred to as 'capitulum' or 'head'). The family Poaceae has a peculiar inflorescence of small spikes (*spikelets*) organised in panicles or spikes that are usually simply and improperly referred to as *spike* and panicle. The genus *Ficus* (Moraceae) has an inflorescence called syconium and the genus *Euphorbia* has *cyathia* (sing. *cyathium*), usually organised in umbels.

5

Ornamental Plant

Ornamental plants or *garden plants* are typically grown in the flower garden or as house plants. Most commonly they are grown for the display of their flowers. Other common ornamental features include leaves, scent, fruit, stem and bark. In some cases, unusual features may be considered ornamental, such as the prominent and rather vicious thorns of *Rosa sericea*. In all cases, their purpose is the enjoyment of gardeners and visitors. Ornamental plants may also be used for landscaping, and for cut flowers.The adequate spacing between pots of plants prevents them from competing for sunlight.

Similarly trees may be called ornamental trees. This term is used when they are used as part of a garden setting, for instance for their flowers, their shapes or for other attractive characteristics. By comparison, trees used in larger landscape effects such as screening and shading, or in urban and roadside plantings, are called *amenity trees*.

For plants to be considered as ornamental, they may require specific work and activity by a gardener. For instance, many plants cultivated for topiary and bonsai would only be considered as ornamental by virtue of the regular pruning carried out on them by the gardener, and they may rapidly cease to be ornamental if the work was abandoned.

Ornamental plants and trees are distinguished from utilitarian and crop plants, such as those used for agriculture and vegetable crops, and for forestry or as fruit trees. This does not preclude any particular type of plant being grown both for ornamental qualities in the garden, and for utilitarian purposes in other settings. Thus lavender is typically grown as an ornamental plant in gardens, but may also be grown as a crop plant for the production of lavender oil.

Other types of ornamental plants include the lily, rose, morning glory and the pink oak.

Garden

A *garden* is a planned space, usually outdoors, set aside for the display, cultivation, and enjoyment of plants and other forms of nature. The garden can incorporate both natural and man-made materials. The most common form is known as a residential garden. Western gardens are almost universally based around plants. Zoos, which display wild animals in simulated natural habitats, were formerly called *zoological gardens*.

The etymology of the word refers to enclosure: it is from Middle English *gardin*, from Anglo-French *gardin*, *jardin*, of Germanic origin; akin to Old High German *gart*, an enclosure. The words *yard*, *court*, and Latin *hortus* (meaning 'garden,' hence horticulture and orchard), are cognates — all referring to an enclosed space.

The term 'garden' in British English refers to an enclosed area of land, usually adjoining a building. This would be referred to as a yard in American English.

Some traditional types of eastern gardens, such as Zen gardens, use plants such as parsley. Xeriscape gardens use local native plants that do not require irrigation or extensive use of other resources while still providing the benefits of a garden environment. Gardens may exhibit structural enhancements, sometimes called follies, including water features such as fountains, ponds (with or without fish), waterfalls or creeks, dry creek beds, statuary, arbors, trellises and more.

Some gardens are for ornamental purposes only, while some gardens also produce food crops, sometimes in separate areas, or sometimes intermixed with the ornamental plants. Food-producing gardens are distinguished from farms by their smaller scale, more labour-intensive methods, and their purpose (enjoyment of a hobby rather than produce for sale). Flower gardens combine plants of different heights, colours, textures, and fragrances to create interest and delight the senses.

Gardening is the activity of growing and maintaining the garden. This work is done by an amateur or professional gardener. A gardener might also work in a non-garden setting, such as a park, a roadside embankment, or other public space. Landscape architecture is a related professional activity with landscape architects tending to specialise in design for public and corporate clients.

Garden design is the creation of plans for layout and planting of gardens and landscapes. Garden design may be done by the garden owner themselves, or by professionals. Most professional garden designers are trained in principles of design and in horticulture, and have an expert knowledge and experience of using plants. Some professional garden designers are also landscape architects, a more formal level of training that usually requires an advanced degree and often a state license. Elements of garden design include the layout of hard landscape, such as paths, rockeries, walls, water features, sitting areas and decking, as well as the plants themselves, with consideration for their horticultural requirements, their season-to-season appearance, lifespan, growth habit, size, speed of growth, and combinations with other plants and landscape features. Consideration is also given to the maintenance needs of the garden, including the time or funds available for regular maintenance, which can affect the choices of plants regarding speed of growth, spreading or self-seeding of the plants, whether annual or perennial, and bloom-time, and many other characteristics.

The most important consideration in any garden design is, how the garden will be used, followed closely by the desired stylistic genres, and the way the garden space will connect to the home or other structures in the surrounding areas. All of these considerations are subject to the limitations of the budget. Budget limitations can be addressed by a simpler garden style with fewer plants and less costly hardscape materials, seeds rather than sod for lawns, and plants that grow quickly; alternately, garden owners may choose to create their garden over time, area by area.

Elements of a Garden

The elements of a garden consist of the following:

Natural conditions and materials:

- Soil
- Rocks
- Light conditions
- Wind
- Precipitation
- Air quality
- Pollution
- Proximity to ocean (salinity)
- Plant materials

Man-made elements:

- Terrace, patio, deck
- Paths
- Lighting
- Raised beds
- Outdoor art/sculpture, such as gazebos and pergolas

- Pool, water garden, or other water elements such as drainage system

Uses for the Garden Space

A garden can have aesthetic, functional, and recreational uses:

- Cooperation with nature
- Plant cultivation
- Observation of nature:
  - Bird-and insect-watching
  - Reflection on the changing seasons
  - Relaxation
  - Family dinners on the terrace
  - Children playing in the yard
  - Reading and relaxing in the hammock
  - Maintaining the flowerbeds
  - Pottering in the shed
  - Basking in warm sunshine
  - Escaping oppressive sunlight and heat
  - Growing useful produce
  - Flowers to cut and bring inside for indoor beauty
  - Fresh herbs and vegetables for cooking

Types of Gardens

Gardens may feature a particular plant or plant type(s):

- Back garden
- Bog Garden
- Cactus garden
- Fernery
- Flower garden

- Front garden
- Herb garden
- Orangery
- Orchard
- Potager
- Rose garden
- Vegetable garden
- Vineyard
- White garden
- Wildflower garden
- Winter garden

Gardens may feature a particular style or aesthetic:

- Alpine or rock garden
- Bonsai or miniature garden
- Children's garden
- Chinese garden
- Dutch garden
- English landscape garden
- French formal garden
- Italian garden
- Japanese garden
- Knot garden
- Mughal garden
- Native garden
- Persian garden
- Roman gardens
- Spanish garden
- Terrarium

- Trial garden
- Tropical garden
- Water garden
- Wild garden
- Xeriscaping
- Zen garden

Types of garden:

- Botanical garden
- Butterfly garden
- Butterfly zoo
- Cold frame garden
- Community garden
- Container garden
- Cottage garden
- Cutting garden
- Garden conservatory
- Greenhouse
- Green wall

Forest garden; Hanging garden; Hydroponic garden; Rain garden; Raised bed gardening; Residential garden; Roof garden; Sacred garden; Sensory garden; Square foot garden; Vertical garden; Walled garden; Windowbox Zoological garden.

6

House Plant

A *house plant* is a plant that is grown indoors in places such as residences and offices. Houseplants are commonly grown for decorative purposes and health reasons such as indoor air purification. Plants used in this fashion are most commonly, though not always, tropical or semi-tropical.

Plant Requirements

Major factors that should be considered when caring for houseplants are moisture, light, soil mixture, temperature, humidity, fertilizers, potting, and pest control. The following includes some general guidelines for houseplant care. For specific houseplant needs, the tags that sometimes come with plants are notoriously unhelpful and generic. Specific care information may be found widely online and in books.

Moisture

Both under-watering and over-watering can be detrimental to a houseplant. The best way to determine whether a plant needs water is to check the soil moisture. Feeling the soil is most reliable, since moisture meters are often inaccurate. Most potted plants must be allowed to reach an appropriate level of dryness in between waterings, though the amount of watering required varies greatly depending on the species. Proper soil moisture can range from still slightly moist on the soil surface to very dry to nearly the bottom of the pot. Watering a plant by the calendar is not recommended. If a plant does need to be watered, water should be slowly poured over the surface of the soil until it begins to drain out the bottom of the pot, ensuring complete saturation. However, sometimes the soil separates from the sides of the pot if it is allowed to dry out thoroughly, allowing the water to flow down the sides of the rootball and out the bottom too quickly to be absorbed and retained by the soil and roots. If this is the case, it may be necessary to set the plant in a shallow dish of water long enough for it to soak up enough water to moisten the rootball to its center. Repotting should eliminate this problem. Repotting should be done only when necessary, since the roots of a plant that is in an excessively large pot may rot.

Through the process of photosynthesis, plants convert the energy in sunlight to chemical energy, which fuels plant growth. The two important factors for providing light to a house plant are *intensity* and *duration*.

Different plants require different light intensities. Intensity (or quality) of light is difficult to measure without a light meter. It is usually measured in units of lux. 100 lux or less is usually considered 'low intensity' or 'indirect' lighting. A bright office has about 400 lux of illumination. 1,000 lux or more is usually considered 'high intensity' lighting. Direct outdoor sunlight is in the range 32,000-1,00,000 lux. Foot-candles are also occasionally used.

The duration of light exposure is as important as the intensity. Quality exposure of 8 to 16 hours is ideal for most plants. Photoperiodism must also be considered, since some plants such as Poinsettia and Schlumbergera are influenced by either decreasing or increasing daylight hours.

Windows are the most common sources of light for houseplants. In the Northern Hemisphere, south-facing windows have the most sun exposure, while western, eastern, and north-facing windows have progressively less exposure. Natural sunlight through windows is affected by seasonal changes, cloud cover, and window treatments. The length of time that light is provided will determine how the plant grows. Providing 16 hours of light/day will promote strong roots, stems and abundant leaves. Decreasing that amount to 12 hours of light/day will signal that the short days of Winter are coming so the plant energy will focus more on flower production and less on green growth.

Artificial light sources can provide an alternative or supplement to window lighting. Fluorescent lighting provides excellent light quality whereas standard incandescent bulbs do little to promote plant growth. 'Cool', or 'blue', fluorescent lights at 6500k provide the light needed for lush green foliage plants, while 'warm', or 'red', fluorescent lights at 3000k provide the light needed for blooming flowers and fruit production. Warm whites are better for flowering plants while cool whites are more suitable for green, leafy growth. When used together, these bulbs are closer to the full spectrum light that comes from the sun, although less powerful.

There are several types of lighting units which can sustain indoor plants. Choosing the best type depends on the need of the plants grown and/or your budget. For the sake of efficiency, incandescents, no matter how cheap, should not be used. Not only do they provide little or no benefit to plants, but the cost of the electricity will outweigh the cost of purchasing multiple incandescent bulbs and fixtures in the long run. Fluorescents are your safest bet. CFL fluorescents are the cheapest option, but more than a couple bulbs are almost always required to be running at once. The next step up is shop lights, available mostly in 2-ft. or 4-ft. fluorescent tubes. The best type of fluorescent are called High Output Fluorescents. Also available in 2-ft and 4-ft. tubes, these bulbs provide more wattage (54 watts each is standard) thus more lumens per watt (92 at the current time). That's about 5,000 lumens per dual 4-ft H.O. Fluorescent Unit. The most serious lights that are used by professionals and in greenhouses as a supplement, are known as Metal Halide or High Pressure Sodium Grow Lights. These lights provide the most lumens, heat and intensity of light so they should be positioned respectively further from the tops of plants to prevent burning.

Soil

House plants are generally grown in specialized soils called *potting compost* or *potting soil*, not in local natural soil. A good potting compost mixture includes soil conditioners to provide the plant with nutrients, support, adequate drainage, and proper aeration. Most potting composts contain a combination of peat and vermiculite or perlite. Concern over environmental damage to peat bogs, however, is leading to the replacement of peat by coir (coconut fibre), which is a sustainable resource. A nutrient rich compost can usually be bought wherever potted plants are sold.

If local natural soil is to be used, it should first be heat sterilized by placing the soil in an oven at 90°C (200°F) for at least 30 minutes. This will ensure that the soil does not contain any harmful bacteria. Most locals soils, especially those with a high proportion of clay, do not drain well enough to be a suitable growing medium for houseplants. Coir or peat is used to increase aeration and make heavy soils more absorbent. Vermiculite and perlite aid in drainage in a soil mixture. Perlite is recommended over vermiculite because it does not break down as easily. A coarse grade sand or grit can be used as a substitute for a drainage mechanism if needed. These three ingredients can be mixed in varying ratios to create different potting soil types. For a plant that requires fast drainage, such as a cactus, use plenty of coarse sand, grit or perlite. For a plant that requires plenty of moisture, use more coir. A good all purpose soil mixture is

2 parts coir and 1 part perlite or vermiculite. A so-called "heavy soil mix" will contain sterilised soil, milled sphagnum moss or coir, and perlite in equal proportions. It is also possible to make a soil mixture that actually contains no soil by mixing equal parts peat moss and perlite (or vermiculite). The soiless mixture will retain more moisture.

Temperature

Most houseplants are tropical species selected for their adaptation to growth in a climate which ranges from 15°C to 25°C (60°F to 80°F), similar to the temperature in most homes. Temperature control for other plants with differing requirements needs attention to heating and/or cooling.

Humidity

Humidity is slightly more difficult to control than temperature. The more commonly used houseplants have established that they can survive in low humidity environments as long as their roots are kept properly irrigated. Most plants thrive in 80 per cent relative humidity while most homes are usually kept around 20 per cent to 60 per cent relative humidity. Besides buying a humidifier, there are a few things that can be done to increase humidity around houseplants. The most popular methods used to raise the ambient humidity are misting and pebble trays, which are shallow trays covered with pebbles and filled with water that evaporates to increase humidity. Other methods of raising humidity include grouping plants closely together and not placing plants in drafty areas. Misting is somewhat controversial among gardeners, with some that swear by it and others that say it does little to increase humidity around plants.

Fertilizers

In a potted environment, soil nutrients can eventually deplete. Adding fertilizer can artificially provide these nutrients. However, adding unnecessary fertilizer can be harmful to the plant. Because of this, careful consideration must be taken before fertilizing. If a plant has been in the same potting mix for a year or more and is no longer thriving, then it may be a candidate for nutrient replacement done by using a complete fertilizer at half the recommended label dilution rate.

Fertilizers are usually marked with a number such as 20-20-20. These numbers indicate the percentages of nitrogen, phosphorus, and potassium respectively, the three elements that are needed in the most quantity for plant growth. Nitrogen is essential for green, leafy growth. Phosphorous is essential for flowering or fruiting plants. Potassium is essential for strong roots and increased nutrient uptake. Numbers higher than 15 are usually man-made, chemical fertilizers. Organic fertilizers have a much lower ratio. A 4-2-2 ratio of these elements is usually good for green foliage plants, while a 2-6-4 ratio is usually better for flowering plants. A complete fertilizer will also include the minor and trace elements, such as calcium, magnesium and iron.

While variation may occur between brands, a general rule is to mix 1 tablespoon to every gallon of water. In all cases, it is better to under-fertilize than over-fertilize. The diluted mixture is then used to water the plants. The growth of the plants should be monitored to determine if the fertilizer is helping or harming, and how often (if at all) it should be used. Schedules can range from every other week to every three months. For convenience, granular, time-released fertilizers are also available.

Pot Types and Sizes

Proper pot size is an important factor to consider. A pot that is too large will cause root disease because of the excess moisture retained in the soil, while a pot that is too small will restrict a plant's growth. Generally, a plant can stay in the same pot for two or so years. Pots come in a variety of types as well, but usually can be broken down into two groups: porous and non-porous. Porous pots are usually clay and are highly recommended because they provide better aeration as air passes laterally through the sides of the pot. Non-porous pots such as glazed or plastic pots tend to hold moisture longer and restrict airflow. Another needed feature is drainage holes. Usually pots come with holes in the bottom to allow excess water to flow out of the soil which helps to prevent root rot. If a pot does not have drainage holes, it is best to double pot that plant so the inner pot can be lifted out and the excess water accumulated in the bottom of the outer pot can be removed. Soak old pots thoroughly in a solution of 1 part bleach to 10 parts water to kill any bacteria that may remain.

Effect on Indoor Air Pollution

Indoor plants reduce components of indoor air pollution, particularly volatile organic compounds (VOC) such as benzene, toluene, and xylene. The compounds are removed primarily by soil microorganisms. Plants can also remove CO2, which is correlated with lower work performance, from indoor areas. The effect has been investigated by NASA for use in spacecrafts. Plants also appear to reduce airborne microbes and increase humidity.

Alternative Growing Methods

Hydroculture

Aside from traditional soil mixtures, media such as expanded clay may be employed in hydroculture, in which the plant is grown in a water and nutrient solution. This technique has a number of benefits, including an odourless, reusable, and more hygienic media. Any habitat for soil-bound pests is also eliminated, and the plant's water supply is less variable. However, some plants do not grow well with this technique, and media is often difficult to find in some parts of the world, such as North America, where hydroponics and specifically hydroculture is not as well-known or widespread.

Sub-irrigation

Sub-irrigation offers another alternative to top-watering techniques. In this approach the plant is watered from the bottom of the pot. Water is transferred up into the potting media (be it soil or others) by capillary action. Advantages of this technique include controlled amounts of water, resulting in lower chances of overwatering if done correctly, no need to drain plants after watering unlike traditional top-water methods, and less compaction of the media due to the pressure put on the media from top-watering.

Indoor Bonsai

Indoor bonsai are bonsai which have been cultivated for the indoor environment. Traditionally, bonsai are shaped from temperate climate trees grown in containers but kept outdoors. Kept in the artificial environment of a home, these trees weaken and die. A number of tropical and sub-tropical tree species will survive and grow indoors. Some of these are suited to bonsai aesthetics and can be shaped much as traditional outdoor bonsai are.

Tropical and Subtropical

- *Aglaonema* (Chinese Evergreen)
- *Amaryllis*
- *Aphelandra squarrosa* (Zebra Plant)
- *Araucaria heterophylla* (Norfolk Island Pine)
- *Asparagus densiflorus* (Asparagus Fern)
- *Begonia* species and cultivars
- *Bromeliaceae* (Bromeliads)
- *Chamaedorea elegans* (Parlour Palm)
- *Chlorophytum comosum* (Spider Plant)
- *Citrus*, compact cultivars such as the Meyer Lemon
- *Dracaena*

for lumber. Some other common uses for them are as soap, varnish, paint, food and perfumes.

Life Cycle

Gymnosperms are spore-bearing plants (sporophytes), with a sporophyte-dominant life cycle; as in all other vascular plants the gametophyte (gamete-bearing phase) is relatively short-lived. Two spore types, microspores and megaspores, are generally produced in pollen cones or ovulate cones, respectively. A short-lived multicellular haploid, gamete-bearing phase (gametophyte) develops inside the spore wall. Pollen grains (microgametophytes) mature from microspores, and ultimately produce sperm cells; megagametophyte tissue develops in the megaspore of each ovule, and produces multiple egg cells. Thus, megaspores are enclosed in ovules (unfertilized seeds) and give rise to megagametophytes and ultimately to egg cells. During pollination, pollen grains are physically transferred between plants, from pollen cone to the ovule, being transferred by wind or insects. Whole grains enter each ovule through a microscopic gap in the ovule coat (integument) called the micropyle. The pollen grains mature further inside the ovule and produce sperm cells. Two main modes of fertilization are found in gymnosperms. Cycads and *Ginkgo* have motile sperm that swim directly to the egg inside the ovule, while conifers and gnetophytes have sperm with no flagella that are conveyed to the egg along a pollen tube. After fertilization (joining of the sperm and egg cell), the zygote develops into an embryo (young sporophyte). More than one embryo is usually initiated in each gymnosperm seed. Competition between the embryos for nutritional resources within polyembryonic seeds produces programmed cell death to all but one embryo. The mature seed comprises the embryo and the remains of the female gametophyte, which serves as a food supply, and the seed coat (integument).

8

Pollination Syndrome

Pollination syndromes are suites of flower traits that have evolved in response to natural selection imposed by different pollen vectors, which can be abiotic (wind and water) or biotic, such as birds, bees, flies, and so forth. These traits include flower shape, size, colour, odour, reward type and amount, nectar composition, timing of flowering, etc. For example, tubular red flowers with copious nectar often attract birds; foul smelling flowers attract carrion flies or beetles, etc. Pollination syndromes are excellent examples of convergent evolution.

The 'classical' pollination syndromes as they are currently defined were developed in the 19th Century by the Italian botanist Federico Delpino. Although they have been useful in developing our understanding of plant-pollinator interactions, an uncritical acceptance of pollination syndromes as providing a framework for classifying these relationships is rather out of date.

Abiotic Pollination Syndromes

These do not attract animal pollinators. Nevertheless, they often have suites of shared traits.

Wind Pollination (Anemophily)

Flowers may be small and inconspicuous, green and not showy. They produce enormous numbers of relatively small pollen grains (hence wind-pollinated plants may be allergens, but seldom are animal-pollinated plants allergenic). Their stigmas may be large and feathery to catch the pollen grains. Insects may visit them to collect pollen; in some cases these are ineffective pollinators and exert little natural selection on the flowers, but there are also examples of ambophilous flowers which are both wind and insect pollinated.

Water Pollination (Hydrophily)

Water-pollinated plants are aquatic and pollen is released into the water. Water currents therefore act as a pollen vector in a similar way to wind currents. Their flowers tend to be small and inconspicuous with lots of pollen grains and large, feathery stigmas to catch the pollen. However, this is relatively uncommon and most aquatic plants are insect-pollinated, with flowers that emerge into the air.

Biotic Pollination Syndromes

Bee Pollination (Melittophily)

Bee-pollinated flowers can be very variable in their size, shape and colouration. They can be open and bowl-shaped (radially symmetrical) or more complex and non-radially symmetric (zygomorphic) such as many peas, foxgloves, etc.

Some bee flowers tend to be yellow or blue, often with ultraviolet nectar guides and scent. Nectar, pollen, or both are offered as rewards in varying amounts. The sugar in the nectar tends to be sucrose-dominated.

There are diverse types of bees, however. Honeybees, bumblebees, orchid bees, etc are large groups that are quite distinctive in size, tongue length and behaviour (some solitary, some colonial). Thus generalization about bees is difficult. Some plants can only be pollinated by bees because their anthers release pollen internally, and it must be shaken out by buzz pollination (also known as 'sonication'). Bees are the only animals that perform this behaviour. Bumblebees sonicate, but honeybees do not.

Bee pollination from mobile beehives is of great economic value for orchards such as apple or almond.

Butterfly Pollination (Psychophily)

Butterfly-pollinated flowers tend to be large and showy, pink or lavender in colour, frequently have a landing area, and are usually scented. Since butterflies do not digest pollen (with one exception), more nectar is offered than pollen. The flowers have simple nectar guides with the nectaries usually hidden in narrow tubes or spurs, reached by the long tongue of the butterflies.

Moth Pollination (Phalaenophily)

Among the more important moth pollinators are the hawk moths (Sphingidae). Their behaviour is similar to hummingbirds: they hover in front of flowers with rapid wingbeats. Most are nocturnal or crepuscular. So moth-pollinated flowers tend to be white, night-opening, large and showy with tubular corollas and a strong, sweet scent produced in the evening, night or early morning. A lot of nectar is produced to fuel the high metabolic rates needed to power their flight.

Other moths (Noctuids, Geometrids, Pyralids, for example) fly slowly and settle on the flower. They do not require as much nectar as the fast-flying hawk moths, and the flowers tend to be small (though they may be aggregated in heads).

Fly Pollination (Myophily and Sapromyophily)

The classical syndromes recognise two types of fly pollination: myophily and sapromyophily. Some flies feed on nectar and pollen as adults (particularly bee flies

(Bombyliidae), hoverflies (Syrphidae), etc.). Those regularly visit flowers. On the other hand, male fruit flies (Tephritidae) are attracted to and feed on specific floral attractant, which acts as fly's sex pheromone precursor or booster, of some wild orchids (Bulbophyllum species — with highly moveable lip) that do not produce nectar. These are the myophiles. Sapromyophiles, on the other hand, normally visit dead animals or dung. They are attracted to flowers that mimic these odoriferous items. They obtain no reward and would quickly leave, but the plant may have traps to slow them down. These plants have a strong, unpleasant odor, and are brown or orange in colour. They are not as common as myophilous plants. Myophilous plants do not tend to have a strong scent, and tend to be purple, violet, blue, and white, open dishes, or tubes. Although they have traditionally been considered to be ineffective and unreliable pollinators, their sheer numbers and the presence of some flies throughout the year make them important pollinators for many plants.

Flies tend to be important pollinators in high-altitude and high-latitude systems, where they are numerous and other insect groups may be lacking.

Bird Pollination (Ornithophily)

Although hummingbirds are the most familiar nectar-feeding birds for North Americans, there are analogous species in other parts of the world: sunbirds, honeyeaters, flowerpeckers, honeycreepers, bananaquits, flowerpiercers, lories and lorikeets. Hummingbirds are the oldest group, with the greatest degree of specialization on nectar. Flowers attractive to hummingbirds that can hover in front of the flower tend to be large red or orange tubes with a lot of dilute nectar, secreted during the day. Since birds do not have a strong response to scent, they tend to be odourless. Perching birds need a substantial landing platform, so sunbirds, honeyeaters, and the like are less associated with tubular flowers.

Bat Pollination (Chiropterophily)

Bat-pollinated flowers tend to be large and showy, white or light coloured, open at night and have strong odours. They are often large and bell-shaped. Bats drink the nectar, and these plants typically offer nectar for extended periods of time. Sight, smell, and echo-location are used to initially find the flowers, and excellent spatial memory is used to visit them repeatedly. In fact, bats can identify nectar-producing flowers using echolocation, a talent that was only recently discovered. In the New World, bat pollinated flowers often have sulfur-scented compounds, but this does not carry to other parts of the world Bat-pollinated plants have bigger pollen than their relatives.

Beetle Pollination (Cantharophily)

Beetle-pollinated flowers are usually large, greenish or off-white in colour and heavily scented. Scents may be spicy, fruity, or similar to decaying organic material. Most beetle-pollinated flowers are flattened or dish shaped, with pollen easily accessible, although they may include traps to keep the beetle longer. The plant's ovaries are usually well protected from the biting mouthparts of their pollinators. Beetles may be particularly important in some parts of the world such as semi-arid areas of southern Africa and southern California and the montane grasslands of KwaZulu-Natal in South Africa.

Biology

Pollination syndromes reflect convergent evolution towards forms (phenotypes) that limit the number of species of pollinators visiting the plant. They increase the functional specialization of the plant with regard to pollination, though this may not affect the ecological specialization (i.e. the number of species of pollinators within that functional group). They are responses to common selection pressures exerted by shared pollinators or abiotic pollen vectors, which generate correlations among traits. That is, if two distantly related plant species are both pollinated by nocturnal moths, for example, their flowers will converge on a form which is recognised by the moths (e.g. pale colour, sweet scent, nectar released at the base of a long tube, night-flowering).

Advantages of Specialization

Efficiency of pollination: the rewards given to pollinators (commonly nectar or pollen or both, but sometimes oil, scents, resins, or wax) may be costly to produce. Nectar can be cheap, but pollen is generally expensive as it is relatively high in nitrogen compounds. Plants have evolved to obtain the maximum pollen transfer for the minimum reward. Different pollinators, because of their size, shape, or behaviour, have different efficiencies of transfer of pollen. And the floral traits affect efficiency of transfer: columbine flowers were experimentally altered and presented to hawkmoths, and flower orientation, shape, and colour were found to affect visitation rates or pollen removal.

Pollinator Constancy: to efficiently transfer pollen, it is best for the plant if the pollinator focuses on one species of plant, ignoring other species. Otherwise, pollen may be dropped uselessly on the stigmas of other species. Animals, of course, do not aim to pollinate, they aim to collect food as fast as they can. However, many pollinator species exhibit constancy, passing up available flowers to focus on one plant species. Why should animals specialize on a plant species, rather than move to the next flower of any species? Although pollinator constancy was recognized by Aristotle, the benefits to animals are not yet fully understood. The most common hypothesis is that pollinators must learn to handle particular types of flowers, and they have limited capacity to learn different types. They can only efficiently gather rewards from one type of flower.

Advantages of Generalization

Pollinators fluctuate in abundance and activity independently of their plants, and any one species may fail to pollinate a plant in a particular year. Thus a plant may be at an advantage if it attracts several species or types of pollinators, ensuring pollen transfer every year. Plants do, in many species, have the back-up option of self-pollination, if they are not self-incompatible.

Criticisms of the Syndromes

Whilst it is clear that pollination syndromes can be observed in nature, there has been much debate amongst scientists as to how frequent they are and to what extent we can use the classical syndromes to classify plant-pollinator interactions. Although some species of plants are visited only by one type of animal (i.e. they are functionally specialized), many plant species are visited by very different pollinators. For example, a flower may be pollinated by bees, butterflies, and birds. Strict specialization of plants relying on one species of pollinator is relatively rare, probably because it can result in variable reproductive success across years as pollinator populations vary significantly. In such cases, plants should generalize on a wide range of pollinators, and such ecological generalization is frequently found in nature. A study in Tasmania found the syndromes did not usefully predict the pollinators.

This debate has led to a critical re-evaluation of the syndromes, which suggests that on average about one third of the flowering plants can be classified into the classical syndromes. This reflects the fact that nature is much less predictable and straightforward than 19th Century biologists originally thought. Pollination syndromes can be thought of as extremes of a continuum of greater or lesser specialization or generalization onto particular functional groups of pollinators that exert similar selective pressures and the frequency with which flowers conform to the expectations of the pollination syndromes is relatively rare. In addition, new types of plant-pollinator interaction, involving 'unusual' pollinating animals are regularly being discovered, such as specialized pollination by spider hunting wasps (Pompilidae) and fruit chafers (Cetoniidae) in the eastern grasslands of South Africa. These plants do not fit into the classical syndromes, though they may show evidence of convergent evolution in their own right.

An analysis of flower traits and visitation in 49 species in the plant genus *Penstemon* found that it was possible to separate bird- and bee- pollinated species quite well, but only by using floral traits which were not considered in the classical accounts of syndromes, such as the details of anther opening. Although a recent review concluded that there is "overwhelming evidence that functional groups exert different selection pressures on floral traits", The sheer complexity and subtlety of plant-pollinator interactions (and the growing recognition that non-pollinating organisms such as seed predators can affect the evolution of flower traits) means that this debate is likely to continue for some time.

9 Pollination

Pollination is the process by which pollen is transferred in plants, thereby enabling fertilization and sexual reproduction. Pollen grains, which contain the male gametes (sperm) to where the female gamete(s) are contained within the carpel; in gymnosperms the pollen is directly applied to the ovule itself. The receptive part of the carpel is called a *stigma* in the flowers of angiosperms. The receptive part of the gymnosperm ovule is called the *micropyle*. Pollination is a necessary step in the reproduction of flowering plants, resulting in the production of offspring that are genetically diverse.

The study of pollination brings together many disciplines, such as botany, horticulture, entomology, and ecology. The pollination process as an interaction between flower and vector was first addressed in the 18th century by Christian Konrad Sprengel. It is important in horticulture and agriculture, because fruiting is dependent on fertilisation, which is the end result of pollination.

Abiotic Pollination

Abiotic pollination refers to situations where pollination is mediated without the involvement of other organisms. Only 10 per cent of flowering plants are pollinated without animal assistance. The most common form, anemophily, is pollination by wind. This form of pollination is predominant in grasses, most conifers, and many deciduous trees. Hydrophily is pollination by water and occurs in aquatic plants which release their pollen directly into the surrounding water. About 80 per cent of all plant pollination is biotic. Of the 20 per cent of abiotically pollinated species, 98 per cent is by wind and 2 per cent by water.

Biotic Pollination

More commonly, the process of pollination requires pollinators: organisms that carry or move the pollen grains from the anther to the receptive part of the carpel or pistil. This is *biotic pollination*. The various flower traits (and combinations thereof) that differentially attract one type of pollinator or another are known as pollination syndromes.

There are roughly 2,00,000 varieties of animal pollinators in the wild, most of which are insects. *Entomophily*, pollination by insects, often occurs on plants that have developed colored petals and a strong scent to attract insects such as, bees, wasps and occasionally ants (Hymenoptera), beetles (Coleoptera), moths and butterflies (Lepidoptera), and flies (Diptera). In *Zoophily*, pollination is done by vertebrates such as birds and bats, particularly, hummingbirds, sunbirds, spiderhunters, honeyeaters, and fruit bats. Plants adapted to using bats or moths as pollinators typically have white petals and a strong scent, while plants that use birds as pollinators tend to develop red petals and rarely develop a scent (few birds have a sense of smell).

Pollination can be accomplished by *cross-pollination* or by *self-pollination*.

Cross-pollination, also called *allogamy* occurs when pollen is delivered to a flower from a different plant. Plants adapted to outcross or cross-pollinate often have taller stamens than carpels or use other mechanisms to better ensure the spread of pollen to other plants flowers.

Self-pollination occurs when pollen from one flower pollinates the same flower or other flowers of the same individual. It is thought to have evolved under conditions when pollinators were not reliable vectors for pollen transport, and is most often seen in short-lived annual species and plants that colonize new locations.

Self pollination may include *autogamy*, were pollen moves to the female part of the same flower; or *geitonogamy*, when pollen is transferred to another flower on the same plant. Plants adapted to self-fertilize often have similar stamen and carpel lengths. Plants that can pollinate themselves and produce viable offspring are called self-fertile. Plants that can not fertilize themselves are called self-sterile, a condition which mandates cross pollination for the production of offspring.

Cleistogamy is self-pollination that occurs before the flower opens. The pollen is released from the anther within the flower or the pollen on the anther grows a tube down the style to the ovules. It is a type of sexual breeding, in contrast to asexual systems such as apomixis. Some *cleistogamous* flowers never open, in contrast to *chasmogamous* flowers that open and are then pollinated. Cleistogamous flowers by necessity are self-compatible or self-fertile plants. Many plants are self-incompatible, and these two conditions are end points on a continuum.

Pollination also requires consideration of pollenizers. The terms 'pollinator' and 'pollenizer' are often confused: a *pollinator* is the agent that moves the pollen, whether it be bees, flies, bats, moths, or birds; a *pollenizer* is the plant that serves as the pollen source for other plants. Some plants are *self-fertile* or *self-compatible* and can pollinate themselves (e.g., they act as their own pollenizer). Other plants have chemical or physical barriers to self-pollination.

In agriculture and horticulture pollination management, a good pollenizer is a plant that provides compatible, viable and plentiful pollen and blooms at the same time as the plant that is to be pollinated or has pollen that can be stored and used when needed to pollinate the desired flowers. *Hybridization* is effective pollination between flowers of different species, or between different breeding lines or populations. see also Heterosis.

Peaches are considered self-fertile because a commercial crop can be produced without cross-pollination, though cross-pollination usually gives a better crop. Apples are considered self-incompatible, because a commercial crop must be cross-pollinated. Many commercial fruit tree varieties are grafted clones, genetically identical. An orchard block of apples of one variety is genetically a single plant. Many growers now consider this a mistake. One means of correcting this mistake is to graft a limb of an appropriate pollenizer (generally a variety of crabapple) every six trees or so.

Evolution of Plant/Pollinator Interactions

Pollination syndromes are flower traits that attract pollinators, and can be highly specialized. Plants and their pollinators are often in co-evolutionary mutualisms.

The first fossil record for abiotic pollination is from fern-like plants in the late Carboniferous period. Gymnosperms show evidence for biotic pollination as early as the Triassic period. Many fossilized pollen grains show characteristics similar to the biotically-dispersed pollen today. Furthermore, the gut contents, wing structures, and mouthpart morphologies of fossilized beetles and flies suggest that they acted as early pollinators. The association between beetles and angiosperms during the early Cretaceous period led to parallel radiations of angiosperms and insects into the late Cretaceous. The evolution of nectaries in late Cretaceous flowers signals the beginning of the mutualism between hymenopterans and angiosperms.

Pollination management is a branch of agriculture that seeks to protect and enhance present pollinators and often involves the culture and addition of pollinators in monoculture situations, such as commercial fruit orchards. The largest managed pollination event in the world is in Californian almond orchards, where nearly half (about one million hives) of the US honey bees are trucked to the almond orchards each spring. New York's apple crop requires about 30,000 hives; Maine's blueberry crop uses about 50,000 hives each year.Bees are also brought to commercial plantings of cucumbers, squash, melons, strawberries, and many other crops. Honey bees are not the only managed pollinators: a few other species of bees are also raised as pollinators. The alfalfa leafcutter bee is an important pollinator for alfalfa seed in western United States and Canada. Bumblebees are increasingly raised and used extensively for greenhouse tomatoes and other crops.

The ecological and financial importance of natural pollination by insects to agricultural crops, improving their quality and quantity, becomes more and more appreciated and has given rise to new financial opportunities. The vicinity of a forest or wild grasslands with native pollinators near agricultural crops, such as apples, almonds or coffee can improve their yield by about 20 per cent. The benefits of native pollinators may result in forest owners demanding payment for their contribution in the improved crop results — a simple example of the economic value of ecological services.The American Institute of Biological Sciences reports that native insect pollination saves the United States agricultural economy nearly an estimated $3.1 billion annually through natural crop production; pollination produces some $40 billion worth of products annually in the United States alone.

Pollination of food crops has become an environmental issue, due to two trends. The trend to monoculture means that greater concentrations of pollinators are needed at bloom time than ever before, yet the area is forage poor or even deadly to bees for the rest of the season. The other trend is the decline of pollinator populations, due to pesticide misuse and overuse, new diseases and parasites of bees, clearcut logging, decline of beekeeping, suburban development, removal of hedges and other habitat from farms, and public paranoia about bees. Widespread aerial spraying for mosquitoes due to West Nile fears is causing an acceleration of the loss of pollinators.

The US solution to the pollinator shortage, so far, has been for commercial beekeepers to become pollination contractors and to migrate. Just as the combine harvesters follow the wheat harvest from Texas to Manitoba, beekeepers follow the bloom from south to north, to provide pollination for many different crops.

Loss of pollinators, also known as Pollinator decline (of which colony collapse disorder is perhaps the most well known) has been noticed in recent years. Observed losses would have significant economic impacts. Possible explanations for pollinator decline include habitat destruction, pesticide, parasitism/diseases, and others.

10

Pollen

Pollen is a fine to coarse powder containing the *microgametophytes* of seed plants, which produce the male gametes (sperm cells). Pollen grains have a hard coat that protects the sperm cells during the process of their movement between the stamens to the pistil of flowering plants or from the male cone to the female cone of coniferous plants. When pollen lands on a compatible pistil of flowering plants, it germinates and produces a pollen tube that transfers the sperm to the ovule of a receptive ovary. The individual pollen grains are small enough to require magnification to see detail.

The Structure of Pollen

Pollen itself is not the male gamete, but each pollen grain contains *vegetative* (non-reproductive) *cells* (only a single cell in most flowering plants but several in other seed plants) and a *generative* (reproductive) *cell* containing two nuclei: a tube nucleus (that produces the pollen tube) and a generative nucleus (that divides to form the two sperm cells). The group of cells is surrounded by a cellulose-rich cell wall called the intine, and a resistant outer wall composed largely of sporopollenin called the exine.

Pollen is produced in the *microsporangium* (contained in the anther of an angiosperm flower, male cone of a coniferous plant, or male cone of other seed plants). Pollen grains come in a wide variety of shapes (most often spherical), sizes, and surface markings characteristic of the species. Pollen grains of pines, firs, and spruces are winged. The smallest pollen grain, that of the Forget-me-not (*Myosotis* spp.), is around 6 µm (0.006 mm) in diameter. Wind-borne pollen grains can be as large as about 90-100 µm. The study of pollen is called palynology and is highly useful in paleoecology, paleontology, archeology, and forensics.

In angiosperms, during flower development the anther is composed of a mass of cells that appear undifferentiated, except for a partially differentiated dermis. As the flower develops, four groups of sporogenous cells form with in the anther, the fertile sporogenous cells are surrounded by layers of sterile cells that grow into the wall of the pollen sac, some of the cells grow into nutritive cells that supply nutrition for the microspores that form by meiotic division from the sporogenous cells. Four haploid microspores are produced from each diploid sporogenous cell called a microsporocyte, after meiotic division. After the formation of the four microspores, which are contained by callose walls, the development of the pollen grain walls begins. The callose wall is broken down by an enzyme called callase and the freed pollen grains grow in size and develop their characteristic shape and form a resistant outer wall called the exine and an inner wall called the intine. The exine is what is preserved in the fossil record.

The pollen wall protects the sperm nucleus while the pollen grain is moving from the anther to the stigma, it protects the vital genetic material from drying out and solar radiation. The pollen grain surface is covered with waxes and proteins, which are held in place by structures called sculpture elements on the surface of the grain. The outer pollen wall prevents the pollen grain from shrinking and crushing the genetic material during desiccation and it is composed of two layers. These two layers are the tectum and the foot layer, which is just above the intine. The tectum and foot layer are separated by a region called the columella, which is composed of strengthening rods. The outer wall is constructed with a resistant biopolymer called sporopollenin. The pollen tube passes through the wall by way of structures called apertures.

Pollen apertures are any modification of the wall of the pollen grain. These modifications include thinning, ridges and pores, they serve as an exit for the pollen contents and allow shrinking and swelling of the grain caused by changes in moisture content. Furrows in the pollen grain are called colpi, which along with pores, are a chief criteria for the identifying pollen classes.

Pollen grains may have furrows, the orientation of which (relative to the original tetrad of microspores) classify the pollen as *colpate* or *sulcate*. The number of furrows or pores helps classify the flowering plants, with eudicots having three colpi (*tricolpate*), and other groups having one sulcus.

Except in the case of some submerged aquatic plants, the mature pollen-grain has a double wall, a thin delicate wall of unaltered cellulose (the endospore or *intine*) and a tough outer cuticularized exospore or exine. The exine often bears spines or warts, or is variously sculptured, and the character of the markings is often of value for identifying genus, species, or even cultivar or individual. In some flowering plants, germination of the pollen grain often begins before it leaves the microsporangium, with the generative cell forming the two sperm cells.

The transfer of pollen grains to the female reproductive structure (*pistil* in angiosperms) is called pollination. This transfer can be mediated by the wind, in which case the plant is described as anemophilous (literally wind-loving). Anemophilous plants typically produce great quantities of very lightweight pollen grains, sometimes with air-sacs.

Non-flowering seed plants (e.g. pine trees) are characteristically anemophilous. Anemophilous flowering plants generally have inconspicuous flowers. Entomophilous (literally insect-loving) plants produce pollen that is relatively heavy, sticky and protein-rich, for dispersal by insect pollinators attracted to their flowers. Many insects and some mites are specialized to feed on pollen, and are called palynivores.

In non-flowering seed plants, pollen germinates in the pollen chamber, located beneath and inside the micropyle. A pollen tube is produced, which grows into the nucellus to provide nutrients for the developing sperm cells. Sperm cells of Pinophyta and Gnetophyta are without flagella, and are carried by the pollen tube, while those of Cycadophyta and Ginkgophyta have many flagella.

When placed on the stigma of a flowering plant, under favourable circumstances, a pollen grain puts forth a pollen tube which grows down the tissue of the style to the ovary, and makes its way along the placenta, guided by projections or hairs, to the micropyle of an ovule. The nucleus of the tube cell has meanwhile passed into the tube, as does also the generative nucleus which divides (if it hasn't already) to form two sperm cells. The sperm cells are carried to their destination in the tip of the pollen-tube.

Pollen as a Carrier of Ecological Information in Plants

A Russian theoretical biologist, Vigen Geodakyan (Geodakian), has suggested that the quantity of pollen reaching a pistillate flower can transmit ecological information and also regulate evolutionary plasticity in cross-pollinating plants. Plentiful pollen indicates optimum environmental conditions (for example a plant that is situated at the centre of its natural range, in ideal growing conditions, with a large number of male plants nearby, and favourable weather conditions), whereas a small amount of pollen indicates extreme conditions (at the borders of its range, with a deficiency of male plants, and adverse weather conditions). Geodakian believes that the quantity of pollen reaching a pistillate flower defines the sex ratio, dispersion and sexual dimorphism of a plant population. High pollen quantity leads to a reduction of these characteristics and stabilization of a population. Small quantity leads to their increase and destabilization of a population.

Dependence of the secondary sex ratio on the amount of fertilizing pollen was confirmed on four dioecious plant species from three families – Rumex acetosa (Polygonaceae), Melandrium album (Cariophyllaceae), Cannabis sativa and Humulus japonicus (Cannabinaceae).

Dependence of offspring phenotype variety on amount of pollen was observed by Ter-Avanesyan in 1949. All three studied species of plants (cotton plant, black-eyed pea, and wheat) showed dependence in the direction forecast by the theory — fertilization with a small amount of pollen resulted in an increase in the diversity of the offspring. Ter-Avanesian writes that as a result of a limited pollination "instead of homogenous sorts we get populations".

Pollen in the Fossil Record

Pollen's sporopollenin outer sheath affords it some resistance to the rigours of the fossilisation process that destroy weaker objects; it is also produced in huge quantities. As such, there is an extensive fossil record of pollen grains, often disassociated from their parent plant. The discipline of palynology is devoted to the study of pollen, which can be used both for biostratigraphy and to gain information about the abundance and variety of plants alive — which can itself yield important information about paleoclimates. Pollen is first found in the fossil record in the late Devonian period and increases in abundance until the present day.

Hay Fever

Allergy to pollen is called hay fever. Generally pollens that cause allergies are those of anemophilous plants (pollen is dispersed by air currents.) Such plants produce large quantities of lightweight pollen (because wind dispersal is random and the likelihood of one pollen grain landing on another flower is small) which can be carried for great distances and are easily inhaled, bringing it into contact with the sensitive nasal passages.

In the US, people often mistakenly blame the conspicuous goldenrod flower for allergies. Since this plant is entomophilous (its pollen is dispersed by animals), its heavy, sticky pollen does not become independently airborne. Most late summer and fall pollen allergies are probably caused by ragweed, a widespread anemophilous plant.

Arizona was once regarded as a haven for people with pollen allergies, although several ragweed species grow in the desert. However, as suburbs grew and people began establishing irrigated lawns and gardens, more irritating species of ragweed gained a foothold and Arizona lost its claim of freedom from hay fever.

Anemophilous spring blooming plants such as oak, birch, hickory, pecan, and early summer grasses may also induce pollen allergies. Most cultivated plants with showy flowers are entomophilous and do not cause pollen allergies. In the US, oak pollen starts to cause problems for sufferers in February and is gone by the end of April.

The percentage of people in the United States that is affected by hay fever varies between a 10 per cent and a 20 per cent, and such allergy has proven to be the most frequent allergic response in the nation. There is certain evidential suggestions pointing out hay fever and similar allergies to be of hereditary origin. Individuals whom suffer of eczema or are asthmatic tend to be more susceptible to develop long-term hay fever.

The most efficient way to handle a pollen allergy is by preventing contact with this coarse powder. Individuals carrying the ailment may at first believe that they have a simple summer cold, but hay fever turns out more evident when the apparent cold does not disappear. The confirmation of hay fever can be obtained after examination by a general physician.

Treatment

Antihistamines: Regularly effective to treat mild cases of hay fever, these type of non-prescribed drugs include loratadine, benadryl and chlorphenamine. They do not prevent the discharge of histamine, but it has been proven that they do prevent a part of the chain reaction activated by this biogenic amine, which considerably lower hay fever symptoms. A side effect of antihistamines is somnolence, therefore, it is recommended not to take these drugs while driving an automobile or during the consumption of alcoholic beverages. Although, the reaction to these medications concerning side effects can vary from person to person.

Decongestants: These drugs can be acquired in different presentations such as tablets or even nasal sprays. Decongestants such as sudafed and drixoral can be acquired as over-the-counter medications. Since an oral decongestant drug is known to raise the blood pressure levels, it is recommended for individuals with hypertension to avoid them. The oral decongestant type can aggravate the symptoms of an enlarged prostate, making the process of urinating more complicated.

Pollen in Human Diets

A variety of producers have started selling pollen for human consumption, often marketed as a food (rather than a dietary supplement). The largest constituent is carbohydrates, with protein content ranging from 7 to 35 per cent depending on the plant species collected by bees.

The U.S. Food and Drug Administration (FDA) has not found any harmful effects of pollen consumption, except from the usual allergies. However, FDA does not allow pollen marketers in the United States to make health claims about their produce, as no scientific basis for these has ever been proved. Furthermore, there are possible dangers not only from allergic reactions but also from contaminants such as pesticides and from fungi and bacteria growth related to poor storage procedures. A manufacturers's claim that pollen collecting helps the bee colonies is also controversial.

In forensic biology, pollen can tell a lot about where a person or object has been, because regions of the world, or even more particular locations such a certain set of bushes, will have a distinctive collection of pollen species. Pollen evidence can also reveal the season in which a particular object picked up the pollen. Pollen has been used to trace activity at mass graves in Bosnia, catch a burglar who brushed against a *Hypericum* bush during a crime, and has even been proposed as an additive for bullets to enable tracking them.

11 Carrion Flower

Carrion flowers or *stinking flowers* are flowers that emit an odor that smells like rotting flesh.

While a typical flower may be stereotyped as a colourful, sweet-smelling structure that attracts insects and rewards them with pollen or nectar, this scenario is somewhat perverted for carrion flowers because of the repulsive nature of the scent to most humans. Carrion flowers attract mostly scavenging flies and beetles as pollinators. Some species may trap the insects temporarily to ensure the gathering and transfer of pollen.

Many plants in the genus *Amorphophallus* (family Araceae) are known as 'carrion flowers'. Titan arum (*Amorphophallus titanum*), which has the world's largest flower head, is also called "carrion flower". Rather than a single flower, the titan arum presents an inflorescence or compound flower composed of a spadix or stalk of small and anatomically reduced male and female flowers, surrounded by a spathe that resembles a single giant petal. This plant has a mechanism to heat up the spadix enhancing the emission of the strong odour of decaying meat to attract its pollinators, carrion-eating beetles and 'flesh flies' (family Sarco-phagidae).

Rafflesia

Flowers of plants in the genus *Rafflesia* (family Rafflesiaceae) emit a repulsive odour, similar to that of decaying meat. This odour attracts the flies that pollinate the plant. The world's largest single bloom is *R. arnoldii*. This rare flower is found in the rainforests of Borneo and Sumatra. It can grow to be 3 feet across and weigh up to 15 pounds. *R. arnoldii* is a parasitic plant on *Tetrastigma* vine, which grows only in primary rainforests with no visible leaves, roots, or stem. It does not photosynthesize, but rather uses the host plant to obtain water and nutrients.

Stapelia

Plants in the genus *Stapelia* are also called 'carrion flowers'. They are small, spineless, cactus-like succulent plants. Most species are native to South Africa, and are grown as potted plants elsewhere. The flowers of all species are hairy to varying degrees and generate the odour of rotten flesh. The colour of the flowers also mimics rotting meat. This attracts scavenging flies, for pollination. The flowers in some species can be very large, notably *Stapelia gigantea* can reach 30 cm (12 inches) in diameter.

Smilax or Nemexia

In North America, the herbaceous vines of the genus *Smilax* are known as Carrion flowers. These plants have a cluster of small greenish flowers. The most familiar member of this groups is *Smilax herbacea*. These plants are sometimes placed in the genus *Nemexia*.

Scent

The sources of the flowers' unique scent is not fully identified, partly due to the extremely low concentration of the compounds (5 to 10 parts per billion), but simple amines present in decaying flesh, the appropriately named putrescine and cadaverine, are known to be present. Dimethyl sulfides, including disulfide and trisulfide have been detected in *Amorphophallus*.

Other Plants with Carrion-scented Flowers

- *Crescentia alata*
- *Sterculia foetida*
- *Hydnora africana*
- *Helicodiceros muscivorus*
- *Dracunculus vulgaris*
- *Lysichiton americanum*
- *Symplocarpus foetidus*
- *Arum maculatum*
- *Aristolochia clematitis*
- Plants in the genus *Asimina*, commonly referred to as Pawpaw.

12

Botanical Garden

Botanical gardens or *botanic gardens* are generally well-tended parks displaying a wide range of plants labelled with their botanical names. They may contain specialist plant collections such as cacti and succulent plants, herb gardens, plants from particular parts of the world, and so on; there may be greenhouses, again with special collections such as tropical plants, alpine plants or other exotic plants. Visitor services often include garden tours, educational displays, art exhibitions, book rooms, open-air theatrical and musical performances and other entertainments.

Botanical gardens are often run by universities or other scientific research organizations and often have associated herbaria and research programmes in plant taxonomy or some other aspect of botanical science. In principle their role is to maintain documented collections of living plants for the purposes of scientific research, conservation, display and education, although this will depend on the resources available and the special interests pursued at each particular garden.

The origin of modern botanical gardens can be traced to European mediaeval medicinal gardens known as physic gardens, the first of these being founded during the Italian

Renaissance in the 16th century. This early concern with medicinal plants changed in the 17th century to an interest in the new plant imports from explorations outside Europe as botany gradually established its independence from medicine. In the 18th century systems of nomenclature and classification were devised by botanists working in the herbaria and universities associated with the gardens, these systems often being displayed in the gardens as educational 'order beds'. With the rapid rise of European imperialism in the late 18th century botanic gardens were established in the tropics and economic botany became a focus with the hub at the Royal Botanic Gardens, Kew, near London.

Over the years botanical gardens, as cultural and scientific organisations, have responded to the interests of botany and horticulture. Nowadays most botanical gardens display a mix of the themes mentioned and more: having a strong connection with the general public there is the opportunity to provide visitors with information relating to the environmental issues being faced at the start of the 21st century, especially those relating to plant conservation and sustainability.

Definition

The role of major botanical gardens worldwide has been considered so broadly similar as to fall within textbook definitions. The following definition was produced by staff of the Liberty Hyde Bailey Hortorium of Cornell University in 1976. It covers in some detail the many functions and activities generally associated with botanical gardens.

> "A botanical garden is a controlled and staffed institution for the maintenance of a living collection of plants under scientific management for purposes of education and research, together with such libraries, herbaria, laboratories, and museums as are essential to its particular undertakings. Each botanical garden naturally develops its own special

(formerly the American Association of Botanic Gardens and Arboreta) and in Australasia there is the Botanic Gardens of Australia and New Zealand (BGANZ).

Historical Development

The history of botanical gardens is closely linked to the history of botany itself. When the botanical gardens of the 16th and 17th centuries changed from medicinal gardens to sites displaying beautiful, strange and new (sometimes economically important) plants from distant lands, and further in the 18th century to sites demonstrating the latest plant classification systems devised by botanists working in the associated herbaria, and then to the modern mix of specialist and eclectic gardens serving many interests of horticulture and botany.

Substantial gardens set aside for economic use or display, containing at least some plants gained by special collection or military campaigns abroad, are known from ancient Egypt, Assyria, and Mexico. In about 2800 BCE Chinese Emperor Shen Nung sent collectors to distant regions searching for plants with economic or medicinal value. Early mediaeval Islamic Spain had gardens, like that of Ibn Wafid's at Toledo in the 11th century, which have been called 'botanical'. It has also been suggested that the Spanish conquest of Mesoamerica influenced the history of the botanical garden as gardens in Tenochtitlan, Nezahualcoyotl, Chalco and elsewhere greatly impressed the invaders as the Aztecs knew many more medicinal plants than did the classical world of Europe.

Physic Gardens

Botanical gardens, in the modern sense, developed from physic gardens, whose main purpose was to grow herbs for medicinal use. Such gardens have a long history. In Europe, for example, Aristotle (384 BCE-322 BCE) is said to have had a physic garden in the Lyceum at Athens, which was used for educational purposes and for the study of botany and this was inherited, or possibly set up, by his pupil Theophrastus, the 'Father of Botany'.

Though these ancient gardens shared some of the characteristics of botanical gardens, the forerunners of modern botanical gardens are generally regarded as being the mediaeval monastic physic gardens that originated after the decline of the Roman Empire at the time of Emperor Charlemagne (742-789 CE). These contained a *hortus,* a garden used mostly for vegetables, and another section set aside for specially-labelled medicinal plants and this was called the *herbularis* or *hortus medicus*—more generally known as a physic garden. These gardens were probably given impetus when Charlemagne issued a capitulary of 73 herbs to be used in the physic gardens of his dominions. Many of these were found in British gardens even though they only occurred naturally in continental Europe, demonstrating earlier plant introduction. Certainly the founding of many early botanic gardens was instigated by members of the medical profession.

Sixteenth Century European Gardens

If a botanical garden is defined by its scientific or academic connection then the first true botanical gardens were established with the revival of learning that occurred in the European Renaissance.

Origin in Southern Europe

The botanical gardens of southern Europe were associated with university faculties of medicine and were founded in Northern Italy at Orto botanico di Pisa (1544), Orto botanico di Padova (1545), Orto Botanico di Firenze (1545) and Orto Botanico dell'Università di Bologna (1568). Here the physicians (referred to in English as apothecaries) delivered lectures on the Mediterranean 'simples' or 'officinals' that were being cultivated in the grounds. Student education was no doubt stimulated by the relatively recent advent of printing and the publication of the first herbals. All of these botanical gardens still exist, mostly in their original form.

Northern Europe

The tradition of these Italian gardens passed into northern Europe where similar gardens were established in the Netherlands (Hortus Botanicus Leiden, 1587; Hortus Botanicus (Amsterdam), 1679), Germany (Alter Botanischer Garten Tübingen, 1535; Leipzig Botanical Garden, 1580; Botanischer Garten Heidelberg, 1597; Herrenhäuser Gärten, Hanover, 1666; Botanical Garden in Berlin, 1672), Switzerland (Botanical Garden Zürich, 1560; Basel, 1589); England (University of Oxford Botanic Garden, 1621; Royal Botanic Garden Edinburgh, 1670; Chelsea Physic Garden, 1673), and in France (Jardin des plantes de Montpellier, 1593; Paris, 1597; Jardin des Plantes, Paris, 1635), Denmark (University of Copenhagen Botanical Garden, 1600); Sweden (Uppsala University, 1655), and also in Spain (Botanical Garden of Valencia (Spanish), 1567).

Beginnings of Botanical Science

During the 16th and 17th centuries the first plants were being imported to these major Western European gardens from Eastern Europe and nearby Asia (which provided many bulbs) and these found a place in the new gardens where they could be conveniently studied by the plant experts of the day. For example, Asian introductions were described by Carolus Clusius (1526-1609) who was director, in turn, of the Botanical Garden of the University of Vienna and Hortus Botanicus Leiden. Many plants were being collected from the Near East, especially bulbous plants from Turkey. Clusius laid the foundations of Dutch tulip breeding and the bulb industry, and he helped create one of the earliest formal botanical gardens of Europe at Leyden where his detailed planting lists have made it possible to recreate this garden near its original site. "The *hortus medicus* of Leyden in 1601 was a perfect square divided into quarters for the four continents, but by 1720 however it was a rambling system of beds, struggling to contain the novelties rushing in" and it became better known as the *hortus academicus*. His *Exoticorum libri decem* (1605) is an important survey of exotic plants and animals that is still consulted today. The inclusion of new plant introductions in botanic gardens meant that their scientific role was now widening as botany gradually asserted its independence from medicine.

In the mid to late 17th century the Paris Jardin des Plantes was a centre of interest with the greatest number of new introductions to attract the public. In England the Chelsea Physic Garden was founded in 1673 as the "Garden of the Society of Apothecaries". The Chelsea garden had heated greenhouses and in 1723 appointed Philip Miller (1722-1770) as Head Gardener. He had a wide influence on both botany and horticulture as plants poured into it from around the world. The garden's golden age came in the 18th century, when it became the world's most richly stocked botanical garden. Its seed-exchange programme was established in 1682 and still continues.

With the increase in maritime trade ever more plants were being brought back to Europe as trophies from distant lands and these were triumphantly displayed in the private estates of the wealthy, in commercial nurseries and in the public botanical gardens. Heated conservatories called 'orangeries', such as the one at Kew, became a feature of many botanical gardens. industrial expansion in Europe and North America resulted in new building skills, so plants sensitive to cold were kept over winter in progressively elaborate and expensive heated conservatories and glasshouses.

The Cape, Dutch East Indies

The 18th century was marked by introductions from the Cape of South Africa — including ericas, geraniums, pelargoniums, succulents and proteaceous plants — while the Dutch trade with the Dutch East Indies resulted in a golden era for the Leiden and Amsterdam botanical gardens and a boom in the construction of conservatories.

Seventeenth Century

At the time of the foundation of these first gardens botany had not become a distinct discipline but was simply a descriptive adjunct to medicine. However, it was in the 17th century that botanical gardens began their contribution to a deeper scientific curiosity about plants.

Royal Botanic Gardens, Kew

The Royal Gardens at Kew were founded in 1760, initially as part of the Royal Garden set aside as a physic garden. William Aiton (1741-1793), the first Curator, was taught by garden chronicler Philip Miller of the Chelsea Physic Garden whose son Charles became first Curator of the original Cambridge Botanic Garden (1762). In 1759 the 'Physick Garden' was planted and by 1767 it was claimed that "the Exotick Garden is by far the richest in Europe". Gardens such as the Royal Botanic Gardens, Kew (1759) and Oratava Acclimatization Garden(Spanish), Tenerife (1788) and the Real Jardín Botánico de Madrid (1755) were set up to cultivate new species returned from expeditions to the tropics; they also helped found new tropical botanical gardens. From the 1770s, following the example of the French and Spanish, amateur collectors were supplemented by official horticultural and botanical plant hunters. This was the great era of European, and especially British, imperialism which was "the means by which ideas, knowledge, styles of economy, politics and goods were given international reach" and justified as the spreading of 'civilization' through 'development' and 'improvement'.

At this time England was importing many woody plants from North America, and the popularity of horticulture had increased enormously encouraged by the horticultural and botanical collecting expeditions overseas fostered by the directorship of Sir William Hooker and his keen interest in economic botany. At the end of the 18th century Kew, under the directorship of Sir Joseph Banks, enjoyed a golden age of plant hunting, sending out collectors to the Southern African Cape, Australia, Chile, China, Ceylon (now Sri Lanka), Brazil and elsewhere, and acting as "the great botanical exchange house of the British empire". From its earliest days to the present Kew has in many ways exemplified botanic garden ideals and is respected worldwide for the published work of its scientists, the education of horticultural students, its public programmes, and the scientific underpinning of its horticulture.

Plant Classification

The large number of plants needing description were often listed in garden catalogues and it was at this time that Carl Linnaeus established the system of binomial nomenclature which greatly facilitated the listing process. Names of plants were authenticated by dried plant specimens mounted on card (a *hortus siccus* or garden of dried plants) that were stored in buildings called herbaria, these taxonomic research institutions being frequently associated with the botanical gardens, many of which by then had 'order beds' to display the classification systems being developed by botanists in the gardens' museums and herbaria. Botanical gardens had now become scientific collections as botanists published their descriptions of the new exotic plants, and these were also recorded for posterity in detail by superb botanical illustrations. In this century botanical gardens effectively dropped their medicinal function in favour of scientific and aesthetic priorities and the term 'botanic garden' came to be more closely associated with the herbarium, library (and later laboratories) housed there than with the living collections — on which little research was undertaken.

Nineteenth Century

The late 18th and early 19th centuries were marked by the establishment of tropical botanical gardens as a tool of colonial expansion (for trade and commerce and, secondarily, science) mainly by the British and Dutch, in India, South-east Asia and the Caribbean. This was also the time of Sir Joseph Banks's botanical collections during Captain James Cook's circumnavigations of the planet and his explorations of Oceania which formed the last phase of plant introduction on a grand scale.

Included in the charter of these gardens was the investigation of the local flora for its economic potential to both the colonists and the local people. Many crop plants were introduced by or through these gardens — often in association with European botanical gardens such as Kew or Amsterdam — and included cloves, tea, coffee, breadfruit, cinchona, sugar, cotton, palm oil and Theobroma cacao (for chocolate). It was during these times that the rubber plant was introduced to Singapore. Especially in the tropics, the larger gardens were frequently associated with a herbarium and museum of economy. The Botanical Garden of Peradeniya had considerable influence on the development of agriculture in Ceylon (now Sri Lanka) where the Para rubber tree (*Hevea brasiliensis*) was introduced from Kew, which had itself imported the plant from South America. Other examples include cotton from the Chelsea Physic Garden to the Province of Georgia in 1732 and tea into India by Calcutta Botanic Garden. The transfer of germplasm between the temperate and tropical botanical gardens was undoubtedly responsible for the range of agricultural crops currently used in several regions of the tropics.

Southern Hemisphere

The first botanical gardens in Australia were founded in the early 19th century (the Royal Botanic Gardens, Sydney, 1816; Royal Tasmanian Botanical Gardens, 1818; the Royal

Botanic Gardens, Melbourne, 1845; Adelaide Botanic Gardens, 1854; and Brisbane City Botanic Gardens, 1855) where the tradition of acclimatization and economic exploitation were soon put into practice. To this list can be added major botanical gardens in New Zealand (Dunedin Botanic Gardens, 1863; Christchurch Botanic Gardens, 1863; Wellington Botanic Gardens, 1868) and South Africa (Kirstenbosch National Botanical Garden, 1913 (site dating to 1848).

United States

The first botanical garden in the United States, Bartram's Garden, was founded in 1730 near Philadelphia and in the same year the Linnaean Botanic Garden at Philadelphia itself. In 1859 the Missouri Botanical Garden was founded at St Louis and is now one of the world's leading gardens specializing in tropical plants. This was one of several popular American gardens including Longwood Gardens (1798), Arnold Arboretum (1872), New York Botanical Garden (1891), Huntington Botanical Gardens (1906), Brooklyn Botanic Garden (1910), and Fairchild Tropical Botanic Garden (1938).

Twentieth Century Civic and Municipal Botanical Gardens

A large number of civic or municipal botanical gardens were founded in the 19th and 20th centuries. These did not develop scientific facilities or programmes but the horticultural aspects were strong and the plants often labelled. They were botanical gardens in the sense of building up collections of plants and exchanging seeds with other gardens around the world, although their collection policies were determined by those in day-to-day charge of them. They tended to become little more than beautifully-maintained parks and were, indeed, often under general parks administrations.

Community Engagement

The second half of the twentieth century saw increasingly sophisticated educational, visitor service and interpretation services. Botanical gardens started to cater for many interests and their displays reflected this, often including botanical exhibits on themes of evolution, ecology or taxonomy horticultural displays of attractive flowerbeds and herbaceous borders, plants from different parts of the world, special collections of plant groups like bamboos or roses, specialist glasshouse collections such as tropical plants, alpine plants, cacti and orchids, as well as the traditional herb gardens and medicinal plants. Specialized gardens like the Palmengarten in Frankfurt (1869), one of the world's leading orchid and succulent plant collections, have been very popular. There was a renewed interest in gardens of indigenous plants and areas dedicated to natural vegetation.

With decreasing financial support from governments, there was an increase in revenue-raising public entertainment including music, art exhibitions, special botanical exhibitions, theatre and film, this being supplemented by the advent of 'Friends' organizations and the use of volunteer guides.

Plant Conservation

Plant conservation, and the heritage value of exceptional historic landscapes, were treated with a growing sense of urgency. Specialist gardens were sometimes given a separate or adjoining site, to display native and indigenous plants.

In the 1970s gardens became focussed on the plant conservation. The Botanic Gardens Conservation Secretariat was established by the IUCN, and the World Conservation Union in 1987 with the aim of coordinating the plant conservation efforts of botanical gardens around the world. It maintains a database of rare and endangered species in botanical gardens' living collections. Many gardens hold ex situ conservation collections that preserve genetic variation. These may be held as: seeds dried and stored at low temperature, or in tissue culture (such as the Kew Millennium Seedbank); as living plants, including those that are of special horticultural, historical or scientific interest (such as those held by the NCCPG in the United Kingdom); or by managing and preserving areas of natural vegetation. Collections are often held and cultivated with the intention of reintroduction to their original habitat. The Centre for Plant Conservation at St Louis, Missouri coordinates the conservation of native North American species.

Many of the functions of botanical gardens have already been dealt with in the sections above, which emphasize the scientific underpinning of botanical gardens with their focus on research, education and conservation. However, as multifaceted organizations all sites have their own special interests. In a remarkable paper on the role of botanical gardens Ferdinand Mueller (1825-1896), the director of the Royal Botanic Gardens Melbourne (1852-1873), stated that "in all cases the objects [of a botanical garden] must be mainly scientific and predominantly instructive". He then detailed many of the objectives that were being pursued by the world's botanical gardens in the middle of the 19th century, when European gardens were at their height. Many of these are listed below to give a sense of the scope of botanical gardens' activities at that time, and the ways in which they differed from parks or what he called 'public pleasure gardens':

- availability of plants for scientific research;
- display of plant diversity in form and use;
- display of plants of particular regions (including local);
- plants sometimes grown within their particular families;
- plants grown for their seed or rarity;
- major timber (American English: *lumber*) trees;
- plants of economic significance;
- glasshouse plants of different climates;

- all plants accurately labelled;
- records kept of plants and their performance;
- catalogues of holdings published periodically.

Research facilities utilising the living collections studies in plant taxonomy examples of different vegetation types student education a herbarium selection and introduction of ornamental and other plants to commerce studies of plant chemistry (phytochemistry) report on the effects of plants on livestock at least one collector maintained doing field work.

Botanical gardens must find a compromise between the need for peace and seclusion, and satisfy the demand for information and visitor services including restaurants, information centres and sales areas that bring with them rubbish, noise and hyperactivity. Attractive landscaping and planting design sometimes compete with scientific interests — with science now often taking second place. Some gardens are now heritage landscapes that are subject to constant demand for new exhibits.

Many gardens now have plant shops selling flowers, herbs and vegetable seedlings suitable for transplanting; many, like the UBC Botanical Garden and Centre for Plant Research and the Chicago Botanic Garden, have plant breeding programmes and introduce new plants to the horticultural trade.

Botanical gardens are still being built, such as the first botanical garden in Oman, which will be one of the largest gardens in the world. Once it is completed and will house the first large scale cloud forest in a huge glasshouse. There has been a remarkable development of botanical gardens in China over recent years including the Hainan Botanical Garden of Tropical Economic Plants South China Botanical Garden at Guangzhou, the Xishuangbanna Botanical Garden of Tropical Plants and the Xiamen Botanic Garden but in developed countries many have closed for lack of financial support, this being especially true of botanical gardens attached to universities.

Botanical gardens have always responded to the interests and values of the day. If a single function were to be chosen from the early literature on botanical gardens it would be their scientific endeavour and, flowing from this, their instructional value. In their formative years botanical gardens were gardens for physicians and botanists but then they progressively became more associated with ornamental horticulture and the needs of the general public. It is by the publications coming out of herbaria and similar facilities that the scientific reputation of a botanical garden is now judged, not by its living collections. The interest in economic plants now has less relevance, and the concern with plant classification systems has all but disappeared, while a fascination with the curious, beautiful and new seems unlikely to diminish.

In recent times the focus has been on creating awareness on danger to ecosystems from human overpopulation and its consequent need for biological and physical resources. Botanical gardens provide an excellent medium for much-needed communication between the world of science and the world at large. Education programmes can help the public develop greater environmental awareness by understanding the meaning and importance of ideas like conservation and sustainability.

13

Growing Cut Flowers

Persons trying to enter the business of growing fresh cut flowers need to realize that it is just that, a business, and needs to be treated as such. Factors to be considered when undertaking this type of business include knowledge of the target market, choice and culture of crops, and management of labour, input costs and resources. Being able to grow and harvest a marketable product will not ensure success.

Markets

The most critical aspect of business is finding a product market. Test market interest by growing some flowers as a hobby and taking samples around to potential clients for a reaction. If there is no interest in the product, there is no reason to continue. Main outlets for cut flowers include wholesale florists, retail florists, farmers markets, roadside stands and pick-your-own operations. Other possible markets include grocery stores, craft fairs, restaurants, corporations and hotels/motels. Using the internet to market is currently a novel approach but should be considered as it will increase the potential consumer base. Transportation may become a larger issue with internet marketing.

When selling directly to businesses, adding value to the product by arranging the flowers in some manner may increase sales. Remember, though, that adding value in this manner will increase labour costs.

Many potential markets exist, limited only by one's imagination. Developing a viable market takes time and effort; a trusting relationship must be built up over time.

Selecting Crops

Once a market has been found and the decision has been made to continue with a cut flower business, the second most important decision to make is what crop to grow. There are many factors to consider but one of the most important is to fit potential crops into the existing growing environment. Labour costs are always high when dealing with floriculture crops, and growing any plant where the conditions are not favourable leads to frustration and higher labour costs. The potential crop should also possess resistance to diseases and pests. The goal should be minimal inputs of pesticides to keep costs under control and for public relation purposes in direct product sales. The plants selected should ideally produce inflorescences on long stems, particularly if the target market is a retail florist. A stem length of 18 inches is often the minimum standard. Other characteristics of an ideal crop are:

- high production per square foot
- ease of harvest
- post harvest life of 7-10 days or longer
- a long production period with repetitive harvests

Annuals, herbaceous perennials, woody plants and bulbs can all be used as cut flowers/foliage. Annuals complete their life cycle in one growing season. Herbaceous perennials and bulbs are those which usually die back to the ground at the end of the growing season and resume growth in the spring. Most hardy, woody plants survive the winter season in the dormant state but do not die back to the ground as the herbaceous perennials do. Production management, harvest, pest and disease control are all different for each of these categories. This is another area where careful decision making is required.

Annuals

Annuals provide growers with the advantage of growing crops that are currently most popular with the consumer. With new crops being grown each season, there is less chance of disease and pest problems. Annuals typically have a longer blooming season than perennials. One potential disadvantage of annuals, however, is the higher cost associated with planting each growing season. Direct seeding would be more cost effective than starting seeds early and transplanting out into the field.

Perennials

One advantage of growing perennials is they do not need to be planted each year. Soil preparation is often more critical, however, since they remain in one area for two years or more. Because of their more permanent status, they have a greater possibility of developing disease and insect problems than annuals do. Some herbaceous perennials may need to be divided and replanted as often as every two years. When dividing, more plants can be propagated from the old ones, which lowers the costs associated with purchasing new plants. Others, such as peonies, do not tolerate disturbance as well. Perennials have a shorter blooming season than many of the annuals, which can be a disadvantage.

Bulbs

Bulbous crops include those that grow from underground parts such as bulbs (specialized leaf tissue), corms (specialized stem tissue), tubers (specialized stem tissue) and rhizomes (underground stems). Because these types of plants usually do not branch much, they can be planted more closely than annuals or other perennials, which can lead to a higher yield per square foot of planting. When used as cut flowers, bulbs are typically treated as an annual and planted new each year. This is in contrast to a garden situation where they would be treated as perennials and left in one spot for more than a year.

Advantages of growing bulbous plants include the ease of harvest of typically leafless stems, closer planting leading to a higher yield per square foot, unique flower forms and a current strong market.

Disadvantages include having to plant each season, a higher cost associated with purchasing bulbs compared to seed, and having to completely remove plant parts from the field to avoid weed problems the following season.

Woody Plants

Currently, woody plants are relative newcomers to the fresh cut floral market. A large potential market exists for just the right product. One advantage that woody plants have over annuals, herbaceous perennials and herbs is the different stages that can be harvested and used. In the winter bare branches with attractive bark or buds could be harvested; spring and summer yield flowering branches; fall provides autumn colours of foliage as well as berries which can be used either fresh or preserved. Woody plants live for many years without needing division or disease and pest management that herbaceous perennials require. Established farm shelter belts or mature landscape plants could yield an abundance of usable material. New plantings, however, may take two years or more to begin yielding a marketable product.

Woody plants carry some disadvantages as well. More knowledge of growth habit is required by the harvester to ensure continued success the following seasons. One important thing to note when harvesting flowering branches is whether or not the particular species blooms on current wood or one-year-old wood. Branching habit will also be affected by the type of pruning done. Because woody plants are relatively new to the fresh cut flower and foliage industry, knowledge on post-harvest care is lacking and it may be up to the grower to experiment and find techniques to contribute to a longer vase life of the product.

Bed Preparations

Soil preparation is very important, especially with perennials which may grow in one spot for two or more years. It is advisable to take soil samples to the local county extension office and obtain an identification of your particular soil type along with an analysis of the nutrient supply in the soil. If necessary, add amendments such as compost to enrich the soil.

Some growers recommend using raised beds to grow cut flowers. Raised beds reduce the probability of saturated field conditions and ease harvest by raising the height of the flowers.

Seeds or Transplants?

When annuals are grown, a decision must be made on whether to purchase established plants or start plants from seed. Both decisions have associated costs. Starting plants from seed requires special equipment and additional space. As a result, costs may be higher than when purchasing plants started by a wholesaler. If perennials are being grown, extra plants can often be propagated from existing ones.

Fast-growing crops like zinnias and marigolds are usually ready for initial harvest starting in late June or early July. These can be direct seeded as soon as the soil is warm enough. Other crops like ageratum, lisianthus, and celosia, should be started in a cold frame and moved out as transplants.

Mulching

Mulching is often recommended as a cultural practice, particularly for water and weed management. If plastic mulch is being used, black is preferred to clear since it keeps weeds from sprouting and tearing the plastic. Other mulches include straw, shredded bark, peat moss, pine needles and shredded leaves. Each type has advantages and disadvantages. The type of mulch used is dependent on cost, availability and preference of the grower. Keeping labour costs down by reducing weeding and watering is crucial in making a profit from these crops.

Watering

A good supply of water is critical in maintaining vigorous plants and quality cut flowers. Many growers of cut flowers recommend drip irrigation (at a rate of 1 gallon per hour) because it is more economical than overhead watering. It also decreases water on the foliage, which lessens chances of fungal diseases developing. Frequency of watering will depend on soil type, weather conditions and crop, but a basic rule of thumb is to give the plants 1 inch of water per week.

Fertilizing

Another important area of growing quality cut flowers is a fertilization programme managed to get maximum benefits at the lowest possible cost. One of the first things a grower of cut flowers should do is get the soil tested to determine what types of nutrients may be in the soil and available to the plants. The local county extension office should be contacted for assistance. Once a soil analysis is made, then a decision on type of fertilizer and mode of application must be made. Timing is often critical to get the best quality crop. Annuals, which supply continued harvests over the course of a season, may benefit from a constant low feed; perennials, which often have a flush of bloom and then stop, would benefit more from an early spring or late fall application to boost overall growth.

There are many application methods. Choice depends on grower preference, type of fertilizer being used and associated costs. Liquid fertilizers can be put through irrigation equipment that may already be in place, while granular types can be incorporated prior to planting or applied as a side dressing.

Pest Control

Pest control can be especially critical with a crop that is purchased directly by the consumer and needs to have a flawless appearance. Many growers of fresh cut flowers prefer to use a minimum of pesticides if any at all. Other growers rely on chemicals to keep pests in check but take care to use relatively 'safe' materials at the lowest possible rates. Managing pests with or without the use of chemicals requires grower knowledge of different pests, their life cycles and best method of control.

To lessen the chance of a major insect wiping out a crop, grow healthy, vigorous plants. Also monitor the crop closely to detect pests as early as possible. Treating 'hot spots' is more cost effective than having to treat an entire crop with an insecticide. Know what insects are likely to attack the current crop and watch the weather, as pests often migrate in from other parts of the country on upper level winds. There are web sites that track movement of certain insects over the course of a growing season. Contact your local county extension agent or university for more information on these programmes.

Choice of chemicals depends on the pest, grower preference, and when the crop is going to be harvested and marketed. It is best to consult with local county extension agents for updates on pesticides currently available for use on cut flowers. Some common materials that many consider organic include insecticidal soaps, pyrethrums (naturally occurring compounds in the plant *Chrysanthemum cinerariaefolium*), Bt (*Bacillus thuringiensis*, a highly selective bacteria which starves the target insect by destroying its gut) and neem (also known as azadirachtin) which is extracted from the seeds of the neem tree (*Azadirachta indica*).

Besides insects, other 'pests' may include gophers, rabbits, and mice. These may be more of a problem on perennials or woody plants that are in the field over winter. Control of these may include the use of poisons or traps, or barriers such as netting or fencing to protect the plants.

Disease Control

Growers need to be aware of how environmental conditions and planting practices can influence disease development. Some common disease problems on cut flowers are leaf spots caused by either fungal or bacterial agents, powdery mildew (fungal) and aster yellows (mycoplasma spread by leafhoppers). If a crop is particularly susceptible to a disease, it should not be grown. In eastern North Dakota, *Limonium sinuata* (notchleaf statice) and *Callistephus chinensis* (China aster) are especially susceptible to aster yellows. The extra care required to keep this in check will decrease profits markedly. Disease forecasting models available on the World-Wide-Web are becoming more common in predicting when outbreaks are likely to occur. An informed grower is often able to avoid serious disease problems by adjusting cultural practices accordingly.

Harvest

Horticulture is typically a labour intensive science. Labour management is critical to reduce costs. Approximately half of direct labour costs are associated with harvesting; well-trained workers can reduce labor costs by as much as 10 per cent. One of the key considerations, is training workers what not to harvest so they can quickly pass over undesirable flowers and harvest the rest. The proper stage of harvest is dependent on the crop. Some flowers such as zinnia and ageratum are best harvested when fully mature. Others, such as roses and gladiolus, will continue to open and need to be harvested before they are fully mature. Still others, such as lilies, can be harvested in the bud stage and still open fully. Harvest in the early morning hours while the flowers' stores of water are highest.

Post-harvest

Once harvested, flowers can either be placed directly into buckets of water containing preservative or dry packed (packed out of water) to be hydrated later. Both methods have advantages and disadvantages. Using buckets with water and preservative will maintain the water level in the crop, but transporting can sometimes be difficult. Transportation is easier with dry packing, but flowers need to be placed into a cooler or put into water as soon as possible to avoid damage from wilt.

Although they add cost to the final product, floral preservatives should be used. The benefits preservatives provide in terms of longevity and quality of the product usually far outweigh any extra costs involved. A general purpose preservative for mainstream cut flowers provide the following benefits:

- adds a nutrient source—usually a 1.5-2 per cent sucrose
- lowers the pH of the water to 3.5-4 which makes it (water) more available to the flowers
- reduces bacterial and fungal growth in the water

Storage

If the product is not going directly to market, storage methods need to be evaluated. Refrigeration is critical to keep flowers looking fresh and to maintain their vase life after purchase. The optimum temperature for storage of the majority of fresh cut flowers is 32-38 F, with a relative humidity of 90-95 per cent. This temperature/humidity combination lowers respiration and transpiration of the flower. It also slows growth of fungus and production of ethylene. These are all components that can shorten the shelf life of cut flowers.

Ethylene

Ethylene is particularly damaging, causing the premature death of 30 per cent of all floral crops. Ethylene is a naturally occurring, gaseous plant hormone that speeds up the aging process of plants exposed to it. It is given off by all higher plants but old, decaying plants emit larger quantities. Fruits, vegetables, car exhaust and cigarette smoke are also sources of ethylene.

Some flowers that are particularly sensitive include *Achillea* (yarrow), *Alstroemeria* (Peruvian lily), *Antirrhinum* (snapdragon), *Dianthus* (carnation) and *Lilium* (lilies).

Symptoms include uniform yellowing of leaves, and flowers or florets that drop off in large quantities.

To prevent ethylene problems, keep fruit and vegetables out of the floral cooler, clean out old and decaying flowers, and disinfect coolers and buckets with a 10 per cent bleach solution (one part bleach to nine parts water) or commercial product. Filters can also be installed into coolers to filter the ethylene out of the air.

Surfaces in the cooler should also be disinfected to keep harmful bacteria and fungi from growing. These will shorten the vase life of cut flowers through production of ethylene. Buckets should be disinfected after each use while all surfaces in the cooler should be thoroughly cleaned about once a week.

Transportation

Transporting the crop from the field to the consumer takes special precautions. One important decision is whether to transport the material in or out of water.

Transporting the cut flowers out of water is termed 'dry-packing' and is practiced by commercial growers who ship their product all over the world. This method eliminates the weight of water in the buckets, but water stress on the flowers is more of a concern.

When shipping flowers dry, ice chips should be packed with the flowers to keep the internal temperature of the box down. A climate controlled truck to keep air cool should also be considered.

Flowers should be fully hydrated and 'pulsed' before they are dry packed. Pulsing refers to the practice of putting flowers into a solution for a short period of time, from a few seconds to a few hours, to extend the vase life. Typically a preservative solution is used as a pulsing agent.

Care needs to be taken when packing flowers to keep petal damage to a minimum. Short distance transportation of flowers may allow for the use of buckets with water. Although harder and heavier to transport, flowers will not become water stressed, which could occur with dry packing. All of these decisions will impact the final cost of the product.

Economics/Pricing

Information about current consumption of the product and market saturation must be known to arrive at a pricing structure.

Americans consume fewer floral products than Europeans and Japanese. About 75 per cent of the floral products purchased in the U.S. are imported from Columbia and Ecuador. However, according to surveys conducted by the Association of Specialty Cut Flower Growers (ASCFG), Americans will readily consume locally grown flowers, especially if they offer quality and uniqueness. Locally grown products have the advantage of being fresher and having less potential damage in shipping and handling. Local growers also have a greater ability to respond to regional expectations. Each provides an advantage for the local market.

When pricing cut flowers, it is important to have a knowledge of the local market and what type of pricing structure is current. Having a close relationship with a local florist may help establishing a pricing guideline. Remember to figure in overhead costs of seed, labour, storage and transportation, but don't price the product so high that it's out of the range of the target market.

If the target market is a local wholesaler, the price may be less than what a retailer would pay, but it is likely the wholesaler would buy in bulk and more product would be utilized. A farmers' market might command a higher price for the product, but less may be sold. Again, deciding what the target market will be is crucial.

Tentative Scenario — Zinnias

Here is a tentative scenario for zinnias, incorporating some of the concepts put forth earlier.

Approximately 1 oz of seeds will yield 1000 plants — direct sowing ½ oz/100 feet.

- Seed germinates in three to five days @ 80-85F, five to seven days @ 70-75F.
- Greatest bloom production when day length is less than 14 hours.
- When soil temperature is 70F or higher, time from direct seeding to harvest is about 6-7 weeks.
- Drip irrigate or hand water; do not irrigate overhead.
- Fertilizer needs should be based on soil test results, but about 1½ to 2 pounds of actual nitrogen is needed per every 1000 square feet of production area. A fertilizer ratio of 1:1:1 for N P K is adequate.
- Transplant or sow two weeks after the first planting, with additional plantings spaced a week apart, for a total of six successive plantings.
- Good production will yield an average of 1.3 stems per square foot per week.
- Harvest during the cool part of the day — early morning or late afternoon when the plants are free of dew. Cut stems as long as possible, and only those flowers that are fully open.
- Place newly harvested stems in a commercial floral preservative. They can be stored in vases at 36-40 F

with 85-90 per cent relative humidity for four days without affecting vase life.

- Insects and diseases include aphids, thrips, caterpillars, scarab beetles, and stem miners; powdery mildew, alternaria leaf blight, and aster yellows.

Additional income from field grown flowers can be realized with market planning, patience, control of costs — especially labour — and attention to quality details. Some key points to remember are to start small and find a market before jumping into it. Also, choose cultivars that will grow best in the area, have 18 inches or greater stem length and possess a long or repetitive bloom time. Flowers sold for market should also have a vase life of at least 7-10 days.

At best, the market is a dynamic target with consumers constantly changing their preferences. To be a continual success, the grower must be willing to shift production to meet consumer preferences.

14

Cut Flowers

Many people enjoy having fresh flower arrangements in their home. With the right plants, it is possible to have fresh cut flowers most months of the year. The tables in this fact sheet list various types of plants along with the approximate time of bloom. The flowering dates of the cut flowers will also vary according to seasonal weather, with an early, warm spring bringing an early bloom. If plants are protected by a building or near a large body of water, their date of bloom will also vary.

How to Successfully Grow Cut Flowers from Your Own Garden!

It is best to cut flowers early in the morning while the buds are still cool. Leave at least 3 sets of leaves on the plant to keep the plant vigorous. Most varieties can be cut when they feel like a large, firm marshmallow or when you observe the first petal move away from the bud. If you feel a hard marble texture when squeezing the bud the bud is still too tight to cut. Each variety can vary in cutting stage. A single bloom must be cut tighter than a double bloom. When cut in too tight of a bud, the flower may not open. When learning stages to cut blooms it is helpful to take some buds in the house to observe if they will open.

Wash and bleach all tools, buckets, and vases to reduce flower contact with bacteria. Place the stems immediately in cool water. Remove all foliage that will be below water level in your final arrangement as foliage will begin to break down under water and give your flowers a shorter vase life. Cut the stem underwater as you are placing it in the arrangement. You will see that a drop of water is still attached to the stem end, keeping it from the air and from drying out.

Keep the flowers out of direct sunlight and heat. Change the water in the vases daily if possible to reduce bacteria count. Flowers shouldn't be refrigerated with fruit as fruit emits ethylene gas that speeds flower maturity.

To hold flowers for a few days, put them in a container of water in a cool, dark place. The optimum holding temperature is 33 degrees, however, refrigerator temperatures will also slow the maturity. Allow 2-3 days for tight buds to open. To hasten opening, place the stems in warm water in a warm place with good light.

Perennials and Hardy Bulbs

Many of the plants will flower over a period of several weeks, particularly if you plant several different cultivars Some types, such as the Coreopsis or Gaillardia, will flower for 6 to 8 weeks, especially if the old bloom is picked off. The biggest display of bloom on all perennials is their first flower of the season The later blooms are more scattered and sometimes on shorter stems. The date of flowering for the cut flowers will vary according to the environment and prevailing weather conditions in the part of country where you live.

April

Wild columbine — *Aquilegia canadensis*

Virginia bluebell — *Mertensia virginica*

Daffodil — *Narcissus* spp.

Wild phlox — *Phlox divaricata*

Tulip — early cultivars and species of *Tulipa*

Long-spurred columbine — *Aquilegia chrysantha*

Sweet-william — *Dianthus barbatus*

May

Leopardbane — *Doronicum caucasicum*

Early daylily — *Hemerocallis flava*

Iris — *Iris* spp.

Peony — *Paeoma* spp.

Globeflower — *Trollius europaeus*

Tulip — Cottage, Breeder, Darwin hybrids of *Tulipa*

June

Achillea — *Achillea ptarmica*

Fernleaf yarrow — *Achillea filipendulina*

Perennial spirea — *Astilbe X arendsii*

Peachleaf bellflower — *Campanula persicifolia*

Canterbury-bells — *Campanula medium*

Mountain-bluet — *Centaurea montana*

Shasta daisy — *Chrysanthemum maximum*

Coreopsis — *Coreopsis grandiflora*

Delphinium — *Delphinium* hybrids

Foxglove — *Digitalis purpurea*

Meadowsweet — *Filipendula hexapetala*

Blanketflower — *Gaillardia aristata*

Daylily — *Hemerocallis aurantiaca*

Coralbells — *Heuchera lithophila; H. sanguinea*

Siberian iris — *Iris sibirica*

Lily — *Lilium* species and cultivars

Maltese cross — *Lychnis chalcedonica*

Beebalm — *Monarda didyma*

Beardtongue — *Penstemon barbatus*

Painted daisy — *Chrysanthemum coccineum (Pyrethrum roseum)*

Carolina lupine — *Thermopsis caroliniana*

July

Butterflyweed — *Asclepias tuberosa*

Blackberry-lily — *Belamcanda chinensis*

Peachleaf bellflower — *Campanula persicifolia*

Globe centaurea — *Centaura macrocephala*

Bugbane — *Cimicifuga racemosa*

Blanketflower — *Gaillardia aristata*

Babysbreath — *Gypsophila paniculata*

Sneezeweed — *Helenium autumnale*

Sunflower heliopsis — *Heliopsis helianthoides*

Daylily — many cultivars

Torchlily — *Kniphofia uvaria*

Gayfeather — *Liatris pycnostachya*

Lily — *Lilium* species and cultivars

Statice — *Limonium latifolium*

Garden phlox — *Philox paniculata*

Black-eyed-susan — *Rudbeckia hirta*

August

Monkshood — *Aconitum napellus*

White mugwort — *Artemisia lactiflora*

Frikart aster — *Aster X Frikartii*

Tube clematis — *Clematis heracleifolia*

Joe-pye-weed — *Eupatorium purpureum*

Blanketflower — *Gaillardia aristata*

Sunflower heliopsis — *Heliopsis helianthoides*

White plantainlily — *Hosta plantaginea*

Gayfeather — *Liatris scariosa*

Lily — *Lilium henryi; L.trigrinium; L.formosanum*

False-dragonhead — *Physostegia virginiana*

Coneflower — *Rudbeckia maxima; R. speciosa*

Perennial black-eyed-susan — *Rudbeckia fulgida*

Goldsturm Showy stonecrop — *Sedum spectabile*

Stokes aster — *Stokesia laevis*

September

Japanese anemone — *Anemone japonica*

New England aster — *Aster novae-angliae*

Fall chrysanthemum — *Chrysanthemum morifolium*

Coreopsis — *Coreopsis grandiflora*

Delphinium — many *Delphinium* cultivars

Mistflower — *Eupatorium coelestinum*

Willowleaf sunflower — *Helianthus salicifolius*

Blue salvia — *Salvia azurea*

October

Fischers monkshood — *Aconitium fischeri*

Tartarian aster — *Aster tataricus*

Fall chrysanthemum — *Chrysanthemum morifolium*

Flowering Annuals

Ageratum — *Ageratum houstonianum* (tall growing varieties)

Snapdragon — *Antirrhinum majus*

Calendula — *Calendula officinalis*

China-aster — *Callistephus chinensis*

Cornflower — *Centaurea cyanus*

Calliopsis — *Coreopsis tinctoria*

Cosmos — *Cosmos bipinnatus*

Larkspur — *Delphinium ajacsis*

Annual gailardia — *Gaillardia pulchella*

Strawflower — *Helichrysum bracteatum*

Feverfew — *Chrysanthemum parthenium*

Annual phlox — *Phlox drummondi*

Annual rudbeckia — *Rudbeckia bicolor*

Mealycup sage — *Salvia farinacea*

Scarlet sage — *Salvia splendens*

Pincushion flower — *Scabiosa atropurpurea*

Tall marigold — *Tagetes erecta*

Mexican sunflower — *Tithonia rotundifolia*

Nasturtium — *Tropaeolum majus*

Tuber verbena — *Verbena venosa*

Pansy — *Viola tricolor*

Zinnia — *Zinnia elegans*

Flowering Shrubs and Trees

Shrubs and trees are also a good source of fresh flowers. In many cases, certain shrubs and trees may have an extended period of bloom in which case they are listed only in the month in which they first begin to flower. Examples include abelia, rose-of-sharon and butterfly bush. Plant different species and cultivars for a long period of flowering.

FLOWERING SHRUBS AND TREES AND THEIR MONTH OF BLOOM

February

Spicebush — *Lindera benzoin*

Japanese witchhazel — *Hamamelis japonica*

Winter jasmine — *Jasminum nudiflorum*

March

Cornelian cherry — *Cornus mas*

Garlandflower — *Daphne cneorum*

Spring heath — *Erica carnea*

Golden bells — *Forsythia x-intermedia; F. ovata; F. suspensa; F. viridissima* and cultivars.

Winter honeysuckle — *Lonicera fragrantissima*

April

Shadblow or shadbush — *Amelanchier canadensis*

Rhododendron — *Rhododendron carolinianum; R. catawbiense; R. maximum* and many cultivars

Azaleas — *Rhododendron* spp.

Flowering quince — *Chaenomeles speciosa*

Flowering dogwood — *Cornus florida*

Star magnolia — *Magnolia stellata*

Flowering crabapples — many *Malus* cultivars

Japanese pieris — *Pieris japonica*

Flowering cherries and plums — many *Prunus* cultivars

May

Fringetree — *Chionanthus virginica*

Dogwood — *Cornus florida*

Hawthorn — *Crataegus oxyacantha*

Deutzia — *Deutzia gracilis*

Pearl bush — *Exochorda racemosa*

Mountain-laurel — *Kalmia latifolia*

Kerria — *Kerria japonica*

Beauty bush — *Kolkwitzia amabilis*

Privet — *Ligustrum ovalifolium*

Rose — many *Rosa* cultivars

Spirea — *Spirea thunbergii*

Lilac — *Syringa vulgaris* and other cultivars

Viburnum — *Viburnum carlesii; V. X. burkwoodii*

Weigela — *Weigela florida* and other cultivars

June

Snowhill hydrangea — *Hydrangea arborescens*

Mockorange — *Philadelphus coronarius*

Anthony Waterer spirea — *Spirea bumalda*

July

Glossy abelia — *Abelia grandiflora*

Butterfly bush — *Buddleia davidii*

Summersweet — *Clethra alnifolia*

Rose-of-sharon or shrub althea — *Hibiscus syriacus*

St. Johnswort — *Hypericum calycinum*

Crapemyrtle — *Lagerstroemia indica*

Smoketree — *Continus coggygria (Rhus continus)*

August

Bushclover — *Lespedeza bicolor*

Chastetree — *Vitex agnus-castus*

October

Witchhazel — *Hamamelis virginiana*

15 Commercial Growing of Cut Flowers

Cut flowers used for decoration have been used in Europe and Asia for centuries and can be seen preserved in works of art. The development of selected varieties and named cultivars has been going on since at least 300-400 AD for chrysanthemums in China, although their introduction to Europe was only in the late 1700s. Roses were depicted in art works from 2000 BC and grown extensively during Roman times. Tulips were grown during the 1450s in Constantinople and eventually took Europe by storm 100 years later during the Dutch bulb trading frenzy. Even now, roses, tulips and chrysanthemums are still the most popular flowers sold at the Dutch flower auctions at Aalsmeer.

The use of Australian plants as cut flowers is much more recent. The early commercial cut flower producers in Australia planted introduced species like tulips, roses and carnations using varieties and technology developed overseas. Until very recently Australian flowers were exclusively harvested from the bush and not cultivated for sale. It is only since the 1970s that interest and resources have been put into establishing native plantation-grown crops in Australia. The first species grown commercially were Geraldton wax and kangaroo paws.

Cut Flower Markets

Before the development of Australian plants there was already some market acceptance for bush harvested lines, and when demand increased it became essential to cultivate and produce reliable quality products. The development of different markets is a slow process but is progressing with Australian plants. There is now a steady demand for natives on the domestic fresh flower market although this is limited by the relatively small population of Australia and the reluctance by many people to spend money on fresh flowers! The growers have therefore turned to export to ensure ongoing income from their fresh flowers. Consumers in Japan and Europe spend considerably more on flowers and their seasons oppose ours here in the Southern Hemisphere producing a market for Australian flowers.

The nature of some Australian flowers like banksias has also allowed for the development of dried, preserved and/or dyed flowers. For example, in Germany dried and dyed banksia flowers are used in cemeteries to provide colour during the winter months.

The markets for Australian native flowers are expanding as interest and knowledge of our plants increases. There is always interest in new products to tempt customers and therefore there has been some effort put into researching species that are not grown commercially. The Rural Industries Research and Development Corporation (RIRDC) has funded many projects researching new cut flower species including *Actinotus, Conospermum, Caustis, Baeckea, Leptospermum, Ixodia, Geleznowia, Ozothamnus, Acacia* and *Chamelaucium.*

Cultivar Development

The development of a new cut flower product often follows a development pattern:

- Flowers are initially bush harvested under licence.

- When the product starts to show potential and there is a demand for the flowers the system then moves towards managed stands in natural areas.
- Usually the crop becomes established in areas where they grow naturally but can be grown intensively in plantations. This coincides with the mass propagation of selected varieties to produce uniform and distinct lines.
- Finally the area of production expands into regions outside the preferred natural habitat for the species, including overseas.
- During the later stages of development, selection of hardy, long stemmed types are usually made and this eventually leads to controlled breeding programmes being established. At this time more extensive work is carried out to understand the cultivation requirements of the crop.

Australian plants commonly used as cut flowers, along with some of the cultivars documented. The majority of these have been created here in Australia although extensive research into *Chamelaucium* cultivation and breeding has been carried out in Israel.

Flannel Flower Development

Flannel flowers can be used as an example of the process of domesticating species for cut flower production. They have been used extensively as cut flowers since the 1800s when stems were harvested from natural stands along the New South Wales' north and central coast. The cultivation of this species by commercial cut flower growers began in the early 1990s and research on the species increased after 1995. The crop is therefore in its infancy after only six years of intensive development. During that time progress has been made into understanding the cultivation requirements and in particular the propagation of *Actinotus helianthi*.

The first stage of most new plant introductions involves the screening of many populations and the consequent selection of the most suitable cut flower varieties. In our work flannel flowers were collected from about 60 populations and there was an amazing variation in the growth habits ranging from 20cm to 150cm high. The taller forms were propagated and these selections were then studied in detail. The adoption of a new species by commercial cut flower growers depends on the ease of propagation and flowering under a variety of conditions. With flannel flowers, the propagation has always been the biggest hurdle to overcome and since 1995 research at Mount Annan Botanic Garden had been carried out to investigate seed germination, cutting production and tissue culture techniques to find a successful and reliable multiplication system.

Initial studies involved seed germination from a wide variety of flannel flower populations collected from the NSW coastal areas. Studies to improve germination included seed storage and dormancy breaking methods like smoke application and seed coat removal. Some success was achieved using a smoked paper (Kirstenbosch Seed Primer) but interestingly the results showed that seed from each population of flannel flowers responds differently. Some seed trials resulted in over 90 per cent germination but this is not reproducible every time.

The work then moved onto assessing cutting production of selected varieties and finally tissue culture of the most preferred lines. Flannel flowers can be produced by softwood to semi-hardwood cuttings taken in autumn and treated with a rooting hormone and under-bench heating. Tissue culture has been used successfully to produce larger numbers of individual selections and a commercial laboratory is now growing a couple of varieties.

The next stage was to determine the cultivation requirements. Studies were carried out at Mount Annan

Botanic Garden to assess the plant density required to optimise the yield of the crop and to assess the effect of slow release fertilisers on potted flannel flowers. For cut flower production two different density approaches could be taken. First, planting at high density (15 cm apart) the crop could be grown as an annual and would produce the highest number of stems per square metre of ground. On the other hand, wider spacing allowed a greater number of stems per plant to be produced and the plants could be cropped for two years. The type of system used depends on the management strategies of the individual grower. Flannel flowers respond well to added fertilisers with significant increases in stem number with increasing application rates of slow release fertilisers (up to $10kg/m^3$ potting mix).During the period 1995 to 1999 two field trials were carried out. The first, involving five NSW growers, compared plants of one selection that had been propagated by cuttings, seed and tissue culture. Generally, seed and tissue cultured plants performed better than cutting grown stock. The second field trial was conducted on 19 properties around Australia in every state except Tasmania and the ACT. The aim was to gain a broad understanding of the soil and climate types suitable for flannel flower production, using four to five selections at each site. Many of the sites were suitable for flannel flowers, particularly along the east coast of Australia and also Western Australia. This trial also identified the areas that still require further study to fully understand the species and establish it as a stable commercial crop.

Future Developments

What is the immediate future of flannel flowers? Well the demand for the cut flowers is high enough to warrant further and continued work. The most immediate problems are finding resistant flannel flowers that can survive in soils containing *Fusarium* pathogens, or perfecting the management of the species to ensure they are not so susceptible to disease. Also the release of named flannel flowers varieties onto the market would ensure a consistent and quality product particularly for export. Finally a system needs to be developed to ensure clonal plants can be produced at a reasonable price and this is likely to be from seed production rather than tissue culture in the future.

Cut flower production using native flowers is a developing industry that is essentially in its infancy. Several species like Geraldton wax and kangaroo paw are well known internationally but many other species like flannel flowers are still to be introduced worldwide. It is a slow process that will continue for many years given the amazing number of potential plants found in our flora.

16

Water Garden

Water gardens, also known as *aquatic gardens*, *backyard ponds* and *garden ponds*, usually referring to a man-made feature, typically combine a pool with aquatic plants and often ornamental fish. Fixed items such as rocks, fountains, statuary, waterfalls and watercourses can be combined with the pool to add visual interest and integration with the local landscape and environment.

They have become popular in recent years. They have also been famous in Chinese and European history.

Types of Water Gardens

A water garden in a private residence.

- Containers
- Man-made ponds
- Natural ponds
- Bogs
- Wild River
- Lakes
- Halka lever

Man-made Ponds

In the sixteenth century, Europe was recovering from the Black Death and towns were growing and prospering again. Renewed interest in Greek thought and philosophy led some aristocrats to reconsider the works of Hero of Alexandria in hydraulics and pneumatics. His devices, such as temple doors operated by invisible weights or flowing liquids, and mechanical singing birds powered by steam, motivated several European princes to create similar clever devices to enhance their public image.

In Italy especially, some princes took things a stage further and constructed large water gardens incorporating mechanical devices in water settings. The best-known is the Villa d'Este at Tivoli, constructed in 1550 AD. A hill presented several fountains and dozens of grottoes, where water-driven figures moved or spouted water. Within 50 years there were imitations all over Europe; the best-known today is the Hellbrunn Palace, full of performing figures (human and animal), fountains that erupt without notice, and a water-powered puppet theatre.

One chooses a spot on the banks of a fast-moving river, and places rocks in the path of the water to make a small waterfall. The rocks interfere with the waterflow, causing splashing and bubbles to form. The water splashing makes a pleasant sound and new habitat for fish, crustaceans and wildlife that feed on the fish and the crustaceans.

The river's water level may vary considerably, so proper location of the rocks requires ingenuity to achieve good aeration from the splashing. Finding a good placement of rocks is similar to arranging a Zen garden or Japanese rock garden. A well-done, intuitive placement of rocks can stimulate a feeling of peace or Zen while also achieving a practical effect, since the splashing water adds valuable oxygen to the river and may prevent hypoxia. The more bubbles formed, the more dissolved oxygen is being placed in the river.

Flora

Typical water garden plants are divided into three main categories: submerged, marginal, and floating.

1. Submerged plants are those that live almost completely under the water, sometimes with leaves or flowers that grow to the surface such as with the water lily. These plants are placed in a pond or container usually 1-2 ft. below the water surface. Some of these plants are called oxygenators because they create oxygen for the fish that live in a pond. Examples of submerged plants are:
   - — Water lily (Hardy and Tropical)
   - — Hornwort (*Ceratophyllum demersum*)
2. Marginal plants are those that live with their roots under the water but the rest of the plant above the surface. These are usually placed so that the top of the pot is at or barely below the water level. Examples of these are:
   - — Iris or Flag
   - — Water-crowfoot (*Ranunculus fluitans*)
   - — Bulrush (*Scirpus lacustris*)
   - — Taro, Elephant Ear, roots for poi (*Colocasia esculenta*)
   - — Arrowhead (*Sagittaria latifolia*)
   - — Lotus (*Nelumbo*)
   - — Pickerelweed (*Pontederia cordata*)

Floating plants are those that are not anchored to the soil at all, but are free-floating on the surface. In water gardening, these are often used as a provider of shade to reduce algae growth in a pond. These are often extremely fast growing/multiplying. Examples of these are:

- Mosquito ferns (*Azolla*)
- Water-spangle (*Salvinia*)
- Water-clover (*Marsilea vestita*)

- Water lettuce (Nile lettuce) (*Pistia stratiotes*)
- Water-hyacinth (*Eichhornia crassipes*)

Some areas of the United States do not allow certain of these plants to be sold or kept as they have become invasive species in warmer areas of the country, such as Florida.

Algae are found in all ponds. There are hundreds of species of algae that can grow in garden ponds but they are only usually noticied when they become abundant. Algae often grow in very high densities in ponds because of the high nutrient levels that are typical of garden ponds. Generally alga attaches itself to the sides of the pond and remains innocuous. Some species of algae, namely the dreaded 'blanket weed' can grow up to a foot a day under ideal conditions and can rapidly clog a garden pond. On the other hand, free floating algae are microcopic and are what cause pond water to appear green.

Grass

Grasses, or more technically graminoids, are monocotyledonous, usually herbaceous plants with narrow leaves growing from the base. They include the "true grasses", of the Poaceae (or Gramineae) family, as well as the sedges (Cyperaceae) and the rushes (Juncaceae). The true grasses include cereals, bamboo and the grasses of lawns (turf) and grassland. Sedges include many wild marsh and grassland plants, and some cultivated ones such as water chestnut (*Eleocharis dulcis*) and papyrus sedge (*Cyperus papyrus*). Uses for graminoids include food (as grain, sprouted grain, shoots or rhizomes), drink (beer, whisky), pasture for livestock, thatch, paper, fuel, insulation, construction, sports turf, basket weaving and many others.

Graminoids are among the most versatile life forms. They became widespread toward the end of the Cretaceous period, and fossilized dinosaur dung (coprolites) have been found containing phytoliths of a variety of grasses that include the ancestors of rice and bamboo. Grasses have adapted to conditions in lush rain forests, dry deserts, cold mountains and even intertidal habitats, and are now the most widespread plant type; grass is a valuable source of food and energy for all sorts of wildlife and organics.

Graminoids are the dominant vegetation in many habitats, including grassland, salt-marsh, reedswamp and steppes. They also occur as a smaller part of the vegetation in almost every other terrestrial habitat.

There are some 3,500 species of graminoids.

Many types of animals eat grass as their main source of food, and are called *graminivores* — these include cattle, sheep, horses, rabbits and many invertebrates, such as grasshoppers and the caterpillars of many brown butterflies. Grasses are also eaten by omnivorous or even occasionally by primarily carnivorous animals.

In the study of ecological communities, herbaceous plants are divided into graminoids and *forbs*, which are herbaceous dicotyledons, mostly with broad leaves.

Plants of this type have always been important to humans. They have been grown as food for domesticated animals for up to 10,000 years. They have been used for paper-making since 2400 BC or before. Now they provide the majority of food crops, and have many other uses, such as feeding animals, and for lawns. There are many minor uses, and grasses are familiar to most human cultures.

Characteristics

The smell of the freshly cut grass is produced mainly by cis-3-Hexenal.

Lawns

In some places, particularly in suburban areas throughout the world, the maintenance of a grass lawn is a sign of a homeowner's responsibility to the overall appearance of their neighborhood. One work credits lawn maintenance to "... the desire for upward mobility and its manifestation in the lawn. As Virginia Jenkins, author of *The Lawn*, put it quite bluntly, 'Upper middle-class Americans emulated aristocratic society with their own small, semi-rural estates.' In general, the lawn was one of the primary selling points of these new suburban homes, as it shifted social class designations from the equity and ubiquity of urban homes connected to the streets with the upper-middle class designation of a 'healthy' green space and the status symbol that is the front lawn".

Many municipalities and homeowner's associations have rules which require lawns to be maintained to certain specifications, sanctioning those who allow the grass to grow too long. In communities with drought problems, watering of lawns may be restricted to certain times of day or days of the week. Some people have allergies to grass.

Grass is important in many sports, notably with those played on fields such as American football, Association football, baseball, cricket, and rugby. In some sports facilities, including indoor domes and places where maintenance of a grass field would be difficult, grass may be replaced with artificial turf, a synthetic grass-like substitute. Sports such as golf, tennis and cricket are particularly dependent on the quality of the grass on which the sport is played.

Cricket

The gray area is the *cricket* pitch currently in use. Parallel to it are other pitches in various states of preparation which could be used in other matches.

In cricket, the pitch is the strip of carefully mowed and rolled grass where the bowler bowls. In the days leading up to the match it is repeatedly mowed and rolled to produce a very hard, flat surface for the ball to bounce off. The quality of the preparation can have a considerable influence on the game; a relatively grassy pitch will favour bowlers and a hard and dryer pitch, with less grass remaining, will typically favor batsmen (at least initially). As the grass dries out and is damaged over the course of the match the pitch's characteristics will change, resulting in batting on the first day of a test match being vastly different to batting on the same pitch after 5 days of play.

Golf

Golf is very dependent on a quality grass surface. Grass on golf courses is kept in three distinct conditions: that of the *rough*, the *fairway*, and the *putting green*. Grass on the fairway is short and even, allowing the player to cleanly strike the ball. Playing from the rough is a disadvantage because the grass is generally much longer, which may affect the flight of the ball. Grass on the putting green is the shortest and most even, ideally allowing the ball to roll smoothly over the surface. An entire industry revolves around the development and marketing of grasses for golf courses.

Herb Garden

The *herb garden* is often a separate space in the garden, devoted to growing a specific group of plants known as herbs. These gardens may be informal patches of plants, or they may be carefully designed, even to the point of arranging and clipping the plants to form specific patterns, as in a knot garden.

Herb gardens may be purely functional, or they may include a blend of functional and ornamental plants. The herbs are usually used to flavour food in cooking, though they may also be used in other ways, such as discouraging pests, providing pleasant scents, or serving medicinal purposes (e.g., a *physic garden*), among others.

A kitchen garden can be created by planting different herbs in pots or containers, with the added benefit of mobility. Although not all herbs thrive in pots or containers, some herbs do better than others. Mint, is an example of herb that is advisable to keep in a container or it will take over the whole garden.

The culinary use of herbs may result in positive medical side-effects. In addition, plants grown within the garden are sometimes specifically targeted to cure common illnesses or maladies such as colds, headaches, or anxiety. During the mediaeval period, monks and nuns developed specialist medical knowledge and grew the necessary herbs in specialist gardens. Now, especially due to the increase in popularity of alternative medicine, this usage is heavily increasing. Making a medicinal garden however, requires a great number of plants, one for each malady.

Herbs grown in herb gardens are also sometimes used to make herbal teas.

Borage is commonly grown in herb gardens; its flowers can be used as a garnish.

Some popular culinary herbs in temperate climates are to a large extent still the same as in the medieval period.

Examples of herbs used for specific purposes (lists are examples only, and not intended to be complete):

- *Annual culinary herbs:* basil, dill, summer savory.
- *Perennial culinary herbs:* mint, rosemary, thyme, tarragon.
- *Herbs used for potpourri:* lavender, lemon verbena.
- *Herbs used for tea:* mint, lemon verbena, chamomile, bergamot, hibiscus sabdariffa (for making karkade).
- Herbs used for other purposes: stevia for sweetening, feverfew for pest control in the garden.

However, herbs often have multiple purposes. For example, mint may be used for cooking, tea, and pest control.

Urban Parks

A park is an area of open space provided for recreational use, usually owned and maintained by a local government. Parks commonly resemble savannas or open woodlands, the types of landscape that human beings find most relaxing. Grass is typically kept short to discourage insect pests and to allow for the enjoyment of picnics and sporting activities. Trees are chosen for their beauty and to provide shade.

The world's first public park is claimed to be the City Park, Budapest, Hungary, which was property of the Batthyány family. In 1808 an Imperial law converted it to the English style. Some years later the Count Batthyány ordered that it should be established as a public park. The second public park in the world is the Peel Park, Salford, England opened on 22 August 1846. Another possible claimant for status as the world's first public park is Boston Common (Boston, Massachusetts, USA), set aside in 1634, whose first recreational promenade, Tremont Mall, dates from 1728. True park status for the entire common seems to have emerged no later than 1830, when the grazing of cows was ended and renaming the Common as Washington Park was proposed (renaming the bordering Sentry Street to Park Street in 1808 already acknowledged the reality).

Parks can be divided into active and passive recreation. Active recreation is that which require intensive development and often involves cooperative or team activity, including playgrounds, ball fields and skateparks. Passive recreation is that which emphasizes the open-space aspect of a park and which involves a low level of development, including picnic areas and trails. Organized football matches take place in parks.

A linear park is a park that has a much greater length than width. A typical example of a linear park is a section of a former railway that has been converted into a park (i.e. the tracks removed, vegetation allowed to grow back). Parks are sometimes made out of oddly shaped areas of land, much like the vacant lots that often become city neighbourhood parks.

Country Parks

In some countries, especially the United Kingdom, *country parks* are areas designated for recreation, and managed by local authorities. They are often located near urban populations, but they provide recreational facilities typical of the countryside rather than the town.

Private Parks

Private parks are owned by individuals or businesses and are used at the discretion of the owner. There are a few types of private parks, and some which once were privately maintained and used have now been made open to the public.

Hunting parks were originally areas maintained as open space where residences, industry and farming were not allowed, often originally so that nobility might have a place to hunt—see mediaeval deer park. These were known for instance, as *deer parks* (deer being originally a term meaning any wild animal). Many country houses in Great Britain and Ireland still have parks of this sort, which since the 18th century have often been landscaped for aesthetic effect. They are usually a mixture of open grassland with scattered trees and sections of woodland, and are often enclosed by a high wall. The area immediately around the house is the garden. In some cases this will also feature sweeping lawns and scattered trees; the basic difference between a *country house's park* and its garden is that the park is grazed by animals, but they are excluded from the garden.

Cottage gardens are always associated with roses: shrub roses, climbing roses, and old garden roses with lush foliage, in contrast to the gangly modern hybrid tea roses. Old cottage garden roses include the Gallica rose, which form dense mounded shrubs 3-4 ft high and wide, with pale pink to purple flowers-with single form to full double form blooms. They are also very fragrant, and include the ancient Apothecary's rose, whose magenta flowers were preserved solely for their fragrance. Another old fragrant cottage garden rose is the Damask rose, which is still grown in Europe for use in perfumes. The damasks grow 6 ft or higher, with gently arching canes that help give an informal look to a garden. Even taller are the Alba roses, which are not always white, and which bloom well even in partial shade.

The Provence rose or *Rosa centifolia* is the full and fat rose made famous by Dutch masters in their seventeenth century paintings. These very fragrant shrub roses grow 5 ft tall and wide, with a floppy habit that is aided by training on an arch or pillar. The centifolia roses have produced many descendants that are also cottage garden favorites, including the moss rose. Unlike most modern hybrids, the older roses bloom on the previous year's wood, so they aren't pruned back severely each year like the modern varieties. Because they don't bloom continuously, like their modern counterparts, they can share their branches with Clematis vines, which use the branches for support. A rose in the cottage garden is not segregated with other roses, with bare earth or mulch underneath—but is casually blended with other flowers, vines, and groundcover.

With the introduction of China roses (*rosa chinensis*) late in the eighteenth century, many hybrids were introduced that had the repeat blooming of the China roses, but maintained the informal old rose shape and flower. These included the Bourbon rose and the Noisette rose, which were added to the rose repertoire of the cottage garden. More recently, hybrid 'English' roses introduced by David Austin have become popular cottage garden-style roses. His shrub roses combine the best traits of modern hybrid tea and floribunda roses, with the old garden roses.

Climbing Plants

Many of the old roses had cultivars that grew very long canes, which could be tied to trellises or against walls. These older varieties are called 'ramblers', rather than 'climbers'. Climbing plants in the traditional cottage garden included

European honeysuckle (*Lonicera periclymenum*) and Traveller's Joy (*Clematis vitalba*). The modern cottage garden includes many Clematis hybrids that have the old appeal, with sparse foliage that allows them to grow through roses and trees, and along fences and arbors. There are also many Clematis species used in the modern cottage garden, including *Clematis armandii, Clematis chrysocoma,* and *Clematis flammula.* Popular honeysuckles for cottage gardens include Japanese honeysuckle and *Lonicera tragophylla.*

Hedging Plants

In the traditional cottage garden, hedges served as fences on the perimeter to keep out marauding livestock and for privacy, along with other practical uses. Hawthorn leaves made a tasty snack or tea, while the flowers were used for making wine. The fast-growing Elderberry, in addition to creating a hedge, provided berries for food and wine, with the flowers being fried in batter or made into lotions and ointments. The wood had many uses, including toys, pegs, skewers, and fishing poles. Holly was another hedge plant, useful because it quickly spread and self-seeded. Privet was also a convenient and fast growing hedge. Over time, more ornamental and less utilitarian plants became popular cottage garden hedges, including laurel, lilac, snowberry, japonica, and others.

Popular flowers in the traditional cottage garden included florist's flowers which were grown by enthusiasts—such as violets, pinks, and primroses–and those grown with a more practical purpose. For example, the calendula, grown today almost entirely for its bright orange flowers, was primarily valued for eating, for adding colour to butter and cheese, for adding smoothness to soups and stews, and for all kinds of healing salves and preparations. Like many old cottage garden annuals and herbs, it freely self-sowed, making it easier to grow and share. Other popular cottage garden annuals included violets, pansies, stocks, and mignonette.

Perennials were the largest group of traditional cottage garden flowers—those with a long cottage garden history include hollyhocks, carnations, sweet williams, marguerites, marigolds, lilies, peonies, tulips, crocus, daisies, foxglove, monkshood, lavender, campanulas, Solomon's seal, evening primrose, lily-of-the-valley, primrose, cowslips, and many varieties of roses.

Today herbs are typically thought of as culinary plants, but in the traditional cottage garden they were considered to be any plant with household uses. Herbs were used for medicine, toiletries, and cleaning products. Scented herbs would be spread on the floor along with rushes to cover odors. Some herbs were used for dying fabrics. Traditional cottage garden herbs included sage, thyme, southernwood, wormwood, catmint, feverfew, lungwort, soapwort, hyssop, sweet woodruff, and lavender.

Planting Design

Planting design requires design judgement combined with a good level of horticultural, ecological and cultural knowledge. It includes two major systems: formal planting design and naturalistic planting design.

The history of planting design is an aspect of the history of gardening and the history of landscape architecture. Planting in ancient gardens was often a mix of herbs for medicinal use, vegetables for consumption and flowers for decoration. Purely aesthetic planting layouts seem to have developed after the renaissance and are clearly shown in late-renaissance paintings and plans. The designs were geometrical and plants were used to form patterns. In the East, naturalistic planting design originated as early as around 200 B.C. in China. In the West, the arrangement of plants in informal groups developed as part of the landscape garden style and was strongly influenced by the picturesque.

A planting plan gives specific instructions, often for a contractor about how the soil is to be prepared, what species are to be planted, what size and spacing is to be used and what maintenance operations are to be carried out under the contract. Owners of private gardens may also use planting plans, not for contractual purposes, as an aid to thinking about a design and as a record of what has been planted. A planting strategy is a long term strategy for the design, establishment and management of different types of vegetation in a landscape or garden.

Planting can be established by directly employed gardeners and horticulturalists or it can be established by a landscape contractor (also known as a landscape gardener). Landscape contractors work to drawings and specifications prepared by garden designers or landscape architects.

Alternative Surfacing

Usually, a smooth expanse of lawn is often considered essential to a garden. However, a textured surface "made up of loose gravel, small pebbles, or wood chips is much more satisfactory visually" than a smooth surface. According to Brookes, creating a relaxed feel to a garden is often done by loose surfacing made up of bark chips, pebbles, gravels; also, the various textures, shapes, sizes, colours, and materials of many different paving elements can contribute to making a garden plan pattern and texture, if they are mixed successfully.

Kitchen Garden or Potager

The traditional kitchen garden, also known as a potager, is a seasonally used space separate from the rest of the residential garden — the ornamental plants and lawn areas. Most vegetable gardens are still miniature versions of old family farm plots with square or rectangular beds, but the kitchen garden is different not only in its history, but also its design.

The kitchen garden may be a landscape feature that can be the central feature of an ornamental, all-season landscape, but can be little more than a humble vegetable plot. It is a source of herbs, vegetables, fruits, and flowers, but it is also a structured garden space, a design based on repetitive geometric patterns.

The kitchen garden has year-round visual appeal and can incorporate permanent perennials or woody plantings around (or among) the annual plants.

Thousands of plant species are cultivated for aesthetic purposes as well as to provide shade, modify temperatures, reduce wind, abate noise, provide privacy, and prevent soil erosion. People use cut flowers, dried flowers and houseplants indoors or in greenhouses. In outdoor gardens, lawn grasses, shade trees, ornamental trees, shrubs, vines, herbaceous perennials and bedding plants are used. Images of plants are often used in art, architecture, humour, language, and photography and on textiles, money, stamps, flags and coats of arms. Living plant art forms include topiary, bonsai, ikebana and espalier. Ornamental plants have sometimes changed the course of history, as in tulipomania. Plants are the basis of a multi-billion dollar per year tourism industry which includes travel to arboretums, botanical gardens, historic gardens, national parks, tulip festivals, rainforests, forests with colourful autumn leaves and the National Cherry Blossom Festival. Venus Flytrap, sensitive plant and resurrection plant are examples of plants sold as novelties.

Scientific and Cultural Uses

Tree rings are an important method of dating in archaeology and serve as a record of past climates. Basic biological research has often been done with plants, such as the pea plants used to derive Gregor Mendel's laws of genetics. Space stations or space colonies may one day rely on plants for life support. Plants are used as national and state emblems, including state trees and state flowers. Ancient trees are revered and many are famous. Numerous world records are held by plants. Plants are often used as memorials, gifts and to mark special occasions such as births, deaths, weddings and holidays. Plants figure prominently in mythology, religion and literature. The field of ethnobotany studies plant use by indigenous cultures which helps to conserve endangered species as well as discover new medicinal plants. Gardening is the most popular leisure activity in the U.S. Working with plants or horticulture therapy is beneficial for rehabilitating people with disabilities. Certain plants contain psychotropic chemicals which are extracted and ingested, including tobacco, cannabis (marijuana), and opium.

Garden Pond

A garden pond is a water feature constructed in a garden, normally either for aesthetic purposes or to provide wildlife habitat. The UK charity Pond Conservation has estimated that there are about two million garden ponds in the UK.

Garden ponds can be excellent wildlife habitats. However, knowing how to make a good wildlife pond in practice is rather a matter of trial and error at present because there is remarkably little reliable information available about how to create good wildlife ponds. Despite the popularity of garden ponds, despite dozens of books and web-sites offering advice about making garden ponds, in fact there have been virtually no studies of garden pond wildlife, the best designs for wildlife ponds or of how garden ponds should be managed to maximise their value for wildlife. As a result of this, advice about the making of ponds for wildlife is plagued by the repetition of a range of myths about ponds. These myths were first identified in the early 1990s by Pond Conservation and described in an article in the magazine *British Wildlife*. The Garden Pond Blog, started by a member of Pond Conservation, aims to dispel some of these myths and help people make better garden (or backyard) ponds.

Although people often say that garden ponds make a great contribution to the protection of freshwater wildlife there is in fact no evidence one way or the other to determine whether this is really the case. This is because there have never been any careful studies made of garden ponds compared to ponds in the rest of the landscape. Because of this garden pond owners have the potential to make many original and valuable observations about the ecology of small waterbodies because so little is known about ponds generally, and specifically about the smallest natural ponds, which garden ponds replicate.

Not everything about garden ponds is good. Although invertebrate animals such as dragonflies and water beetles, and amphibians can colonise new ponds quickly, garden ponds also cause problems. In particular, garden ponds can be pathways for the spread of invasive non-native plants. In the UK the non-native species Crassula helmsii and Myriophyllum aquaticum, which cause considerable practical problems in protecting freshwaters, are both escapees from garden ponds.

Ponds may be created by natural processes or by people; however, the origin of the hole in the ground makes little difference to the kind of wildlife that will be found in the pond. Much more important is whether the pond is polluted or clean, how close it is to other wetlands and its depth, particularly whether it dries out from time to time and how many fish (if any) there are.

Naturally, ponds vary more in their physical and chemical conditions from day to day, and even during the day, than other freshwaters, like rivers. People often install pumps in garden ponds to counter these natural tendencies, particularly to maintain higher levels of dissolved oxygen: although this is probably not necessary for wildlife generally, it may be essential to keep fish in a small pond. For ponds with polluted nutrient-rich tapwater added to them, filters can be used to reduce the abundance of algae.

Ponds outside of gardens are fed by five main water sources: rain, inflows (spring, streams, ditches), groundwater and surface runoff. The wildlife value of ponds is greatly affected by the extent to which these water sources are polluted: the less pollution the better. Garden ponds are often filled with tap water; since water supplied for drinking often has high levels of nutrients which, when too abundant, pollute the pond, this gets the pond off to a bad start. Chemical pond treatments said to maintain the 'ecological balance' in ponds have rarely been carefully tested to assess their effects: although some of these treatments may have beneficial effects (for example, adding chalk to a pond polluted by phosphorus could precipitate the nutrient from the water and prevent it from being taken up by algae) most freshwater scientists would not currently consider these an effective solution to pond management problems.

Garden ponds are generally not fed by inflows or groundwater, except in the biggest gardens. Usually the pond will be filled by a combination of rainwater and surface runoff and lost to evaporation. One can make a garden pond/ koi pond that generally ranges in size from 150 gallons to around 10,000 gallons. However, if evaporation exceeds the amount of water added from rain or surface runoff, the pond may dry out during summer. This is not harmful biologically because many freshwater plants and animals (perhaps half of all species) are well adapted to periods of drought, and worldwide so-called 'temporary ponds' (ponds which usually dry out once a year) are an important natutral habitat type. However in a garden, a pond which dries out in summer may be a bit disappointing for the owner since this is the time when most people will be spending time enjoying their pond. And of course some animals, particularly fish, cannot survive periods of drought. Indeed, drought is nature's way of telling fish they are not wanted in a particular place! Amphibians, on the other hand, often benefit from ponds which dry out because this removes the major predators of tadpoles and newtpoles (fish) and, provided the larvae emerge before the pond dries out, the drought presents no problems for the amphibians.

In soils which lack natural clay, additional water loss to drainage and permeation is prevented by a liner. Pond liners are PVC or EPDM foils that are placed between the soil of the pond bed and the water. Liners can also be made from puddled clay, and ponds on free-draining soils can even be self-sealing with fine sediments washed into the pond.

Index